SECRET RICHES

Linda Ball, now based in Singapore, is a freelance journalist and author. She currently writes mainly for Overseas Missionary Fellowship.

SECRET RICHES

Hope among the Handicapped of Hong Kong

LINDA BALL

with
Valerie Conibear and Wendy Blackmur

MarshallPickering
An Imprint of HarperCollins*Publishers*

Marshall Pickering is an Imprint of
HarperCollins*Religious*
Part of HarperCollins*Publishers*
77–85 Fulham Palace Road, London W6 8JB

First published in Great Britain
in 1992 by Marshall Pickering

1 3 5 7 9 10 8 6 4 2

A catalogue record for this book is
available from the British Library

ISBN 0 551 02600 6

Printed and bound in Great Britain by
HarperCollinsManufacturing Glasgow

'I will give you . . . riches stored in secret places, so that you may know that I am the Lord.'

ISAIAH 45:3

The telling of this story is dedicated to the adoptive families of those children who have left the Home of Loving Faithfulness to be so generously embraced by their care and love.

Truthfulness has been our watchword as we have written this account, and honesty our guideline. Truths sometimes hurt and, indeed, there have been tears in the telling. We are truly sorry if any reader suffers undue hurt, but our defence is that we have striven after truth. In the interests of lessening hurt some of the names have been changed, but none of the facts.

Contents

	Foreword	9
	Prelude at Po Leung Kuk	11
1	The Story Begins with "Mama" – and Valerie's Call	13
2	Wendy – Seeking and Finding	21
3	Face to Face – a Firm Friendship	28
4	Clouds – and a New Calling	34
5	Training, Turmoil – and Homecoming	40
6	A Place with Potential	45
7	Early Battles	52
8	Three More Children	59
9	And Two More Make Eight	67
10	And Two Teenagers Make Ten	74
11	Operation Cheung Chau – and Andrew's Adoption	81
12	Painful Disharmony – and More About Suzie	86
13	Plus Five Make Fifteen – and Wendy Makes a Decision	96
14	Dearest to your Heart	103
15	Faith and Finance	108
16	To Valerie – a Daughter	115
17	A Committed and Caring Companion	124
18	God-Given Families	134
19	Building for the Future	145

Contents

20 Community Life – Lasting Friendships
   and some Misunderstandings   153
21 Daniel and His Many Lions   159
22 The Oldest Arrival – and Two More
   Young Ones   171
23 Love for Thomas the Unwelcome Twin   180
24 Hard Questions On Healing and
   True Value   190
25 The Love Goes On   198
26 A Footnote on the Future   205

Foreword

An embarrassing place to visit. But she was keen, so we acquiesced.

We drove there on one of those acid bright December afternoons in which Hong Kong excels. The hard sunlight drew sharp lines on hills and horizon, and bounced off the road in puffs of dust. The cityscape was far behind. Here nothing reminded us of the picture postcard skyscrapers and wonderland tinselled shopping arcades. Here were bare hillsides and an odour of manure. Shacks besieged by scuttling hens and ducks. An extravagance of bush and bloom that encroached onto the narrow roads.

Past a rundown rattan factory and an unimposing building surprisingly signposted in English "Kwu Tung Village Office", Gillian pointed off to the right, to a billboard, a bus and a building.

"Jesus Christ is Lord" proclaimed foot-high letters on a wall pressed close to the roadside. Hardly had I recovered from this incongruity when another claimed my attention. A blue and yellow bus stood in a garden. A double decker bus with curtains and an extra corrugated iron roof. A bus with potplant-lined steps up to a door.

And the building. Its two storeys were blanched by the sunshine, battered and peeling. A wide verandah at ground level and a large balcony above hinted at some former glory.

But its present glory? This was the Home of Loving Faithfulness, a Home for the severely mentally and physically handicapped run by two English ladies, a Chinese nurse and a handful of local staff. There *was* glory there – I sensed it as I was introduced and shown around. As I nodded my head and listened and tried desperately to ask intelligent questions, its glory began to invade my heart right there and then.

So when a year and a half later God asked me to become a volunteer helper at the Home, I didn't question His wisdom or doubt the blessing that would be mine in obedience.

That sun-filled afternoon, though, I tasted the horror of inadequacy. God, I breathed, there's no way I could do what's done here. My mother-in-law, who was with us, reached out in compassion and touched the twisted limbs and I loved her for it and knew myself cold of heart and fearful.

But since then I have found out that distortion of body can house beauty of personality. And I've learnt some things. Like the value of a smile. The preciousness of a laugh. The transience of flesh and bone. The foreverness of a soul. The optimism that there is in a confidence that every forever soul trusting in Jesus will one day be united with a perfect body and mind.

"And he shall wipe all tears from their eyes."

During my time at the Home of Loving Faithfulness I slowly became aware of a story that needed to be told. To be true to the God whose work this Home really is, I seek to unfold this story according to the honour of its name — lovingly and faithfully.

Linda Ball
1992

Prelude at Po Leung Kuk

The entrance hall was chilled with marble and dark wood. A regiment of gilt-framed benefactors looked down on the two young women in light summer dresses who shifted their feet and waited.

A clipped footstep, a jangle of keys and the lady superintendent appeared, unsmiling, to perform her duty of showing the visitors round.

So began an hour on an unsuspecting date in the calendar of the 1960s that was to generate a vision and a calling for the decades to come.

Yet there were no trumpet fanfares. Just sad remembrances.

The austere Po Leung Kuk Children's Home stood aloof in its own walled grounds surprisingly close to the bustling heart of Hong Kong Island. Later, Valerie and Wendy retained no recollection of most of the children in the Home. For after a cursory tour the superintendent, apparently on a whim, decided to show them another part of the building which housed those children never shown to the public.

Unlocking several doors she led them into a large room where, squatting or lying on rows of mats and low cots, were the retarded children, hurt in mind and twisted in body.

It was not the grotesquely angled limbs, not the senseless moans, not the pungent smell of urine – none of these things made it a place of heartbreak. Rather it was the blankness of the children's eyes and the total lack of any response that broke the hearts of the two women.

The children were cleanly dressed in their drab uniform

gowns and were reasonably fed and safely kept, albeit in the most barren and colourless surroundings. But the pain of seeing more than 50 faces unlit with any expression in their eyes or smile on their lips was a feeling they were to recall repeatedly in years to come as one of their most devastating experiences.

Valerie and Wendy left Po Leung Kuk tearful but challenged. Both women were committed Christians and vowed together that they would earnestly pray for these and other mentally and physically handicapped children.

"Father God, please, in your mercy, bring people to love and care for the handicapped children of Hong Kong." They recorded their requests in the prayer diaries they kept by their bedsides.

The heart of God the Father breaks, too, for the handicapped, the orphaned, the rejected, the unloved, and the unwanted. He was waiting to answer the prayers of the two women – using them.

ONE

The Story Begins with "Mama" – and Valerie's Call

Of course, Po Leung Kuk wasn't quite the beginning of our story. How did these two young women come to be living and working in colonial Hong Kong in the 1960s, long before the skyscrapers, international banks and glittering shopping malls made it a centre for finance, trade and tourism?

In a way it all began some thirty years before with a wonderful, bespectacled old-style missionary called Mildred Dibden who was lovingly and respectfully called "Mama" by literally hundreds of Chinese orphans. Her story has been told elsewhere. Relying totally on a prayer-answering God to meet the family's daily needs, Miss Dibden cared for abandoned children in an era when an extra mouth to feed was an intolerable burden on the desperately poor, uneducated farmers and fishermen of Hong Kong. Throughout the Japanese occupation she braved threats of personal assault and defied the worst ravages of wartime deprivation. Her orphanage survived these tyrannies, but not the imperious command of a British committee who took it out of her hands in the 1950s.

Undaunted and true to her calling, Miss Dibden began again, taking in more babies, often weak and sickly, that were abandoned in public places and on her own doorstep. It was when her family numbered 76 that she accepted an offer of help from a young English nursery nurse called Valerie Conibear.

In many ways Valerie's early life made her a natural candidate for the mission field. As a child she heard about relatives who were missionaries in China and Africa. And

13

she found her own heroes and heroines in the stories of other real-life missionaries such as Mary Slessor and David Livingstone. Her grandfather, a Methodist minister to whose home she was evacuated during the war years, often talked to her about Jesus.

After training as a nursery nurse Valerie worked for five years in a children's home in her home area of Portsmouth, then moved to caring for babies awaiting plastic surgery in an orthopaedic hospital.

Honouring her upbringing, the young Valerie, though possessed of a healthy sense of fun and a lively good humour which found an outlet in all kinds of pranks, was serious about Christianity. She read her Bible, prayed every day, and found a certain satisfaction – but "something was lacking".

Leaving the hospital, Valerie worked in a home for orphans and disturbed children from Naval families near Havant. After a year and a half and in response to the sense of restlessness that she expressed to her Methodist minister one Sunday, she applied to and was accepted by the National Children's Homes, to work in the babies section of a large home near Portsmouth.

This was not directly the answer to her growing sense of dissatisfaction, but it did bring her into contact with a number of staff who were committed Christians. One of these, Mabel Roberts, the gentle lady in her fifties who was the headmistress of the school for handicapped children, confronted Valerie with her need to know Jesus Christ in a personal way.

"I had known the Gospel all my 25 years, but I had never asked Jesus to be my Saviour," Valerie recalls.

One afternoon, sitting at tea with Miss Roberts, Valerie realised that being a Christian was not the heritage of an upbringing. It was a personal identification of her sin with the Cross of Christ. It was a heart commitment entered into through repentance and owning of a divine lordship.

That momentous decision inspired her with a new desire to serve God. Should she become a missionary? Perhaps she could train to be a deaconess? It was a period of pushing doors — but as yet not one stood open.

The autumn of 1959. Maureen, also on the staff of the children's home, went to hear a talk on Hong Kong by an Oxfam worker. She returned enthused. The speaker had told her about a missionary called Miss Dibden who ran a home for abandoned children.

Maureen decided to write immediately to offer her help. But even as she repeated the scanty details of the Shatin Babies Home and reached for pen and paper, Valerie was seized with an inexplicable intuition that it was to be her — Valerie — who should go to Hong Kong to do this work.

For a whole anxious month this inner "calling" grew stronger. How could Valerie break this news to Maureen, so positive in her ambition to fill the need herself?

One evening Valerie determined to be honest about her conviction. With an effort of courage she left her room to find Maureen, only to bump into her friend in the corridor.

"I was just coming to talk to you. . . about that babies home in Hong Kong," Valerie faltered.

Maureen's look was rueful. "Exactly what I was coming to talk to you about. I've heard I've failed the medical. My polio, you know. I shan't be able to go, after all. But, Valerie, I've been thinking. At the back of my mind all along has been the idea that maybe this calling isn't for me, anyway. I wonder if God wants you to go. . .?"

Valerie didn't hesitate to write to Miss Dibden, sharing her career experiences and pouring out her feelings. From then on things happened remarkably quickly. The missionary encouraged her, her family was fully supportive, and soon her passage was booked on a cargo passenger ship leaving Birkenhead in January 1960.

SAILING EASTWARDS

En route to the mysterious Orient! Valerie took a disarmingly simple, even naive, view of her great adventure.

"I had no preconceived ideas about Hong Kong. I was going to serve the Lord and I knew there would be difficulties."

This matter-of-fact acceptance came from an inner certainty that she was in God's will. Having harboured thoughts of being a missionary for many years, even before her conversion, this was in many ways the realisation of a dream. Now, standing on the deck of the Blue Funnel Line ship she remembered with a smile her early childish prayers – "Please, God, don't call me to India or Africa. . . I really hate snakes!" Since her conversion no such exemption clauses clouded her thinking.

The ship sailed into Hong Kong – the "Fragrant Harbour" – on a beautiful clear March morning, just after sunrise. Valerie, invited onto the bridge, stared at the dozens of bobbing sampans in the water and the bustle of activity on the dockside. It was already hot and humid; tiny swirls of mist rolled over the water.

Valerie's first view of Miss Dibden approaching along the quayside was as she was so frequently seen – striding briskly amid a bunch of small, bobbing dark heads. Miss Dibden, then in her fifties, was a firm, determined figure of a woman with spectacles on her round face and curly hair continually escaping from the roll at the nape of her neck. With the missionary's customary disregard for fussiness, she dressed simply but neatly – floral print dresses in summer, sweaters and sensible skirts on cooler days. She never wore trousers. Nor the rubber "flip flop" sandals that were virtually part of the local costume; whatever the temperature her definite step was always made in strong, laced leather shoes or sturdy buckled sandals. However, her appearance was far from stern. Though plainly not someone to be trifled with, the disciplined features also betrayed warmth, a motherly gentleness and a very real sense of humour. She was respected, but also deeply loved.

And all those children! Each with the same identical severe haircut, beneath which were big solemn brown eyes, infectious giggles, little pinafores, and skipping feet.

For the children it was a day for an outing, for meeting their new "aunty" and for treats. There was ice cream all round on board ship – courtesy of the captain! Valerie returned the shy smiles of the half dozen or so chattering little girls who were her reception committee. How would she ever tell them apart?

Those whose only images of Hong Kong are of its overcrowded, cramped, high-rise blocks, of its concrete and glass monuments to the gods of money, or of its marbled and gilded comforts devoted to the affluent tourist, may be somewhat surprised to discover that even the Hong Kong of the 90s has its quiet leafy byways, its peaceful sun-dappled beaches. Even more so the Hong Kong of the 60s, which was still largely untouched by big business and consumerism.

Barely half an hour's ride from the noisy, bustling docks and streets of Kowloon, Valerie found herself feasting her fascinated eyes on the luxuriant green scenery of the New Territories, that more rural area of Hong Kong north of the famous Lion Rock landmark. Not far past the less well-known Amah Rock, travelling in the direction in which that sightless stone lady gazes out to sea as she longs for her lost husband, is a small craggy outcrop which in those days overlooked the estuary and a straggling settlement of fishing and farming homes.

Atop this little hill was a rambling building with a chequered career. Some time police station and jail, it now housed the "Yip Family", alias Shatin Babies Home, later renamed, with the natural process of time, Shatin Children's Home.

Anxious to meet her new family, Valerie found the walk up the steep hill in the heat a tiring one. Rather to her distress she found she was not allowed to carry her own luggage. The various trunks and boxes, plus the new typewriter she had bought in Liverpool before leaving, were all assigned to a number of tiny Chinese *amahs* or servants, and the gardener. Her protests were brushed aside. This was Asia and this was the way things were done here and she would, in time, learn to accept it. So she did, eventually – but not quickly or easily.

Her arrival caused quite a stir.

"Swarms of children came to meet me, all looking so bright-eyed, cleanly-dressed and well fed. There were 76 of them – 70 girls and six boys, girl babies being of less value in the Chinese culture and therefore far more likely to be abandoned."

The building, in spite of its age and ill-planned construction with little runs of steep stairs everywhere, was clean and light. Valerie's room, in the oldest part of the house, was a very basic provision – just an iron bedstead with a mosquito net, an old-fashioned wooden desk and a wardrobe.

Although she was the first westerner to come to High Rock to help Miss Dibden, she quickly fitted into family life and her new duties. She taught English classes and presided over the tables at mealtimes. She was responsible for a little dispensary and dealt with coughs and colds, grazed knees and tummy upsets. She took care of visitors, of which there were many, all curious to see what these missionary ladies were up to with their charming if enormous family. The children seemed to thrive on this kind of attention and it had become a tradition for them to put on a nativity play each Christmas for quite a large audience.

Valerie also wrote letters for Miss Dibden, sending news about the Home to supporters from near and far who prayed and provided for the children. And her sewing skills were put to good use, brightening up the rather spartan surroundings with new curtains and upholstery. She was given one half day off each week and on Sunday mornings was allowed out to attend the morning service held at Pui Ying College in Kowloon. She loved the life and never once felt lonely or homesick.

She developed a particular friendship with Miss Leung, the "Bible woman", who taught Scripture lessons. In spite of the cultural and age gaps – Miss Leung was in her late 50s – they became close friends. Valerie found her more approachable than Miss Dibden, so they spent a lot of time together – praying, studying the Bible, and Miss Leung teaching Valerie the local language of Cantonese.

Comments in duplicated letters to supporters showed how readily the newcomer had been accepted by the "Yip Family".

"Valerie," Miss Dibden wrote, "is teaching the eight- to ten-year-olds to do housework in return for pocket money put away safely in plastic money boxes week by week. Occasionally 20 cents is taken out to buy fruit or other things they see in the Shatin market." And Miss Dibden had news to share that would eventually affect the Home's future: "We have been notified by the Social Welfare Officer that there is now a new legislation regarding babies found abandoned. They are, from now on, wards of the Social Welfare Officer. This means that I can no longer take in these babies as my children and be a mother to them."

The big-hearted missionary comments, "This does not disturb me! I'm glad that the welfare of these babies who have been abandoned will, in future, be in the care of the Welfare Officer. It is a great step forward and I only hope the next step will be that there will be new legislation granting these children a given surname on their birth certificate. At the present time they have just a name such as Precious Pearl, nothing more, for nothing more is known about them except the fact that they were abandoned, and the details as to where they were found. Needless to say, a birth certificate with no surname is an embarrassment and a great distress to the young people when they grow older, and presents many difficulties.

"Regarding the Home here and speaking for myself — I realise that I cannot go on indefinitely taking in newly born babies who require so much of my attention. I must, D.V., give more time to the careful training of the 76 now in the family. Valerie and I both feel that we should give the children more of ourselves — to take them out, to teach them English and to encourage in them Christian principles."

And Miss Dibden concludes her letter: "It is hard work here with so many little ones to care for, few luxuries, and very little time to call our own, but for all that it is a most satisfying work, a precious responsibility which we hold from God Himself, and for which He provides all that is needed. Our joy and our reward is to be able to serve Him, and to know that He receives and blesses our service."

Valerie was responsible for replying to the many letters of encouragement generated by the newsletters. However, not many months passed before Miss Dibden handed Valerie a letter which would need a different kind of reply. The postmark was Rutland, England. She read it curiously. It was from a young girl called Wendy. . .

TWO

Wendy – Seeking and Finding

If Valerie's early years could sensibly claim to be a likely background for a missionary, the same could not be said about Wendy's.

For if Wendy thought about it at all, she dismissed religious faith as an irrelevance. As a child her ambition was to be a nurse – unrealised because of a difficult family situation. Her father was an unpredictable man plagued with bouts of depression and even an attempted suicide, which led to several periods of treatment in a mental hospital. Wendy abandoned thoughts of further education, leaving school at 14 to earn a wage to help her mother. Three years later her parents separated and she and her mother moved from Kent to Oxfordshire.

Here Wendy continued a career in accounts. This she did without resentment; she found she even enjoyed it, even though from time to time she thought wistfully about nursing. Essentially a practical, down-to-earth young woman, it was perhaps surprising when she began to feel an unaccountable but definite longing to go to Hong Kong.

Was it just that she was an impressionable 18-year-old touched by the stories she read in the newspapers about the thousands of refugees from China fleeing to Hong Kong at that time? Whatever the cause, her family and friends soon became quite tired of her apparent obsession with this strange place half way round the world.

"I felt a tremendous love for the Chinese people – even though I didn't know a single one! I admired them and felt I really wanted to help them. I had a growing desire to go to Hong Kong. Somehow, I felt my destiny lay there. People got sick of me talking about going to Hong Kong!"

Aged 20, Wendy got a new job and moved to Rutland. Ostensibly, her life was successful. She had good prospects, enjoyed her work and was well liked for her committed and responsible attitude. After the turbulent years of her childhood the lovely thatched cottage which she shared with a friend and later with her mother seemed her first real home. She loved it and its countryside setting. Outwardly self-confident, she was really quite shy and she enjoyed the privacy the cottage afforded her.

But, all through the four years spent there, Wendy's thoughts were still continually on Hong Kong. She felt sure that there her life was to find true fulfilment.

But how? The Hong Kong of which she caught tantalising glimpses on the TV screen was so far away. She wrote to Hong Kong companies, but it seemed no one wanted an accounting machine operator. One day, idly browsing through a magazine, her eye was caught by pictures of Chinese toddlers peering out of rows of cots. The accompanying article told of an English missionary working among abandoned and orphaned children in Hong Kong. Perhaps, Wendy thought, this Miss Mildred Dibden would let her unofficially adopt and financially sponsor one of these Hong Kong babies?

So she wrote the letter that found its way into Valerie's hands.

Valerie, replying as part of her duties at High Rock, wrote back that such sponsorship was not usual, but she also gave news of the Home and the children, and mentioned the current needs "for your prayers".

And Wendy, not knowing at all the God whom she now addressed, did indeed pray in response to Valerie's friendly letter. She wrote back and a regular correspondence between the two girls was established. And although Wendy at first never dreamed of working at the Home, the suggestion inevitably surfaced in time.

Miss Dibden had natural reservations. Her response

was kindly, written with genuine sincerity and concern, but there was no way that she could take into the work someone who was not a committed Christian. It was a Christian missionary work, after all.

Miss Dibden went on to say that she would be visiting London briefly and would be giving a slide show and talk about the Home. Wendy was invited.

But first Wendy met "Aunty Donny". Archdeacon Donithorne and his wife had been the first westerners to go into Hong Kong's infamous Walled City; they were the founders of the West China Evangelistic Band and friends of Miss Dibden. Meeting Mrs Donithorne for lunch in London, Wendy's emotions ran high. Tears dropped onto her untouched meal. "I know I'm meant to be in Hong Kong," she cried.

Wendy wanted Hong Kong. But there was something else now. She wanted to know God in the same way that Miss Dibden and Valerie and Aunty Donny did.

Meeting Miss Dibden a few weeks later, Wendy had a long conversation with her in which it was not difficult for the missionary to recognise the inner strugglings and longings of a heart searching for purpose – and for God.

The London hall was packed that evening for the slide show. As Miss Dibden showed part of the new wing at the Shatin Home, she glanced back over her shoulder. "And, if you come, Wendy, this will be your room."

Her words thrilled Wendy.

That weekend Wendy was surprised to find herself, with Miss Dibden's introduction, staying with some missionaries on furlough and talking with them. She could see that she didn't have the faith they had. That much was clear. As she left, a fragment of a Bible reading went with her: "For I am the Lord, your God, who takes hold of your right hand and says to you, Do not fear; I will help you."

BREAKTHROUGH

Some weeks later she was spending a lonely and restless Sunday at the cottage. She sat watching the morning service on TV. A Birmingham clergyman was speaking about how to have faith in God and he was encouraging those watching to kneel and make a commitment at home. Was this what you did to find God? Wendy knelt down but her heart still felt empty and sad.

By the evening, still disconsolate, she turned on the radio. A song from a modern passion play was being played. Wendy had read about the controversial *A Man Dies* in the newspapers. The Christ in the play wore jeans and a torn T-shirt as he carried his Cross – which many found quite scandalous. The girl singer was called Valerie Mountain. "Valerie" and "Mountain" immediately meant Valerie and the hills of Hong Kong to Wendy, so her attention was caught and she listened.

> Jesus Christ, wise and good,
> They nailed him to a cross of wood.

Suddenly the words made wonderful sense. "Right then and there I knew that Jesus Christ died because of me and for me. And I wanted to follow him."

The elation of that June evening breakthrough carried Wendy floating as on a cloud for several weeks. She understood very little about being a Christian. She went along to her local church the next Sunday, but concentration on the service proved hard. Her heart and mind were soaring up into the rafters of the lofty roof. The words the congregation sang soared upwards, too.

> Praise to the Lord, the Almighty,
> The King of Creation. . .
> Hast thou not seen
> How thy heart's wishes have been
> Granted by what He ordaineth.

It seemed to her that God was saying "yes" to her heart's desire – to go to Hong Kong. And she couldn't wait for the fulfilment.

Wendy wrote to Miss Dibden, trying to tell her what was happening. It wasn't easy; she didn't have the terminology to explain it all. She didn't know the relevant phrases, like "being born again".

But Miss Dibden recognised the experience if she didn't identify the vocabulary. Wendy had made a commitment to Jesus Christ and was His child. Now her request to come to Hong Kong was an entirely different proposition. She wrote back immediately to the effect that Wendy should have a medical checkup and start packing. And, amazingly to Wendy, she quoted the same Bible verse from Isaiah 41 that had recently meant so much: "For I am the Lord, your God, who takes hold of your right hand and says to you, Do not fear; I will help you."

Wendy realised from the beginning that, in spite of her many years of experience, there was a loving humility and acceptance about Miss Dibden that was to make her a perfect example and teacher for the determined new convert.

Dream was becoming reality. Not easily – it was difficult to leave behind a mother who was so dependent on her. But Wendy's baby faith insisted "God will take care of her for me" and, indeed, her mother's security and future were amazingly provided for.

Plans progressed. Through regular correspondence with Valerie, Wendy began to get a mental picture of the Shatin Children's Home and to see how she would fit in. It was decided that she would take over the correspondence and accounts, as well as the English classes, leaving Valerie free to concentrate on the under-fives and more domestic matters.

These early letters established a firm friendship between the two young women. Valerie wrote honestly, describing the difficulties as well as the joys of working at the Home. She was anxious that Wendy, as such a new Christian, would face problems. Miss Dibden wasn't always the easiest person to work for. In as many ways as she could, Valerie did her best to prepare Wendy for life in Hong Kong. And Wendy recognised that Valerie, older by a few years and, more importantly, a person of considerable background in Christian experience, would be able to teach her much about the missionary life that she had chosen.

Wendy's farewells to England proved considerably more stressful than Valerie's, with her tearful mother hardly reconciled to her departure. On the way to the ship at Birkenhead, the car broke down and precious minutes were spent in a garage fixing the problem. Wendy paced up and down in the forecourt, impatient and fearing that she would dissolve into tears. She peered round the corner of the jumbled workshop. An old radio on a shelf announced: "Five to ten: a story, a hymn and a prayer." She listened, idly. The organ played a few bars and in came the choir, singing, "Praise to the Lord, the Almighty, the King of Creation. . ." She let out a long breath and relaxed. It was going to be all right.

The ship's berth was a dreary, deserted place, and it was a cold, miserable, overcast day. But, with the emotional stress of farewells behind her, Wendy thoroughly enjoyed the sea voyage, experiencing a rising anticipation as the *Clytoneus* covered the miles eastward, docking in Hong Kong on 20th February, 1962 – a year and 11 months after Valerie had done so.

So intently had Wendy studied Hong Kong in books and TV programmes, that it had a familiarity which put her immediately at ease. "The only thing that surprised me was the washing – quilts, towels and assorted clothing – hanging on poles and railings even in Nathan Road and other main streets. Hong Kong had already become such a part of me. I never experienced any homesickness!"

In spite of the great differences in their backgrounds, Wendy's first impressions of Hong Kong mirrored Valerie's: the warm reception, the long climb up the hill with the uncomfortable awareness of her luggage being carried by willing bodies so much slighter than her own, and the confusion of dozens of little faces, all apparently identical! What a delicious moment it was when, the following morning, Wendy lay awake in her room soon after the 6am bell, listening to the chattering from the dormitories on either side of her.

"'. . .Aunty Wendy. . . Aunty Wendy. . .!' I could hear my name and knew I was being thoroughly discussed from all angles!"

THREE

Face to Face – a Firm Friendship

Valerie was a little taken aback by her first sight of Wendy. Comfortable in the role of the competent young business woman, Wendy was slim, self-assured and well-groomed. Her long straight mid-brown hair was immaculately coiled on her head. Her grey-blue eyes were framed by squarish heavy-rimmed glasses and – yes – Valerie was sure that she was wearing make-up. And as for those high, high heels. . .

Wendy loved high heels – but soon found them impractical for her new life.

Did Wendy feel she had met a "country mouse" in Valerie?

"No, definitely not! Valerie was very attractive and so natural - there wasn't a hint of artificiality about her."

Tall and slim, Valerie had a serious face, with warm hazel-brown eyes which would suddenly be lit by a lovely and generous smile. Her bobbed dark hair was already greying though she was still in her early 30s. Although she was reserved in temperament – the traumatic death of her mother when she was 12 perhaps responsible for making her cautious about being openly demonstrative – Wendy soon discovered Valerie had a great sense of fun. Their early friendship was sealed many times over in laughter. From the start they worked well together, seeming to perfectly complement each other's strengths and weaknesses.

Wendy soon established herself as the leader in practical matters. But, though finding it far easier to take the initiative and to make decisions than Valerie, Wendy relied much on the stability, serenity and wisdom of her new friend.

Particularly, it was a time for Wendy of establishing herself in her newfound faith and learning Christian principles. Previously she had always done things her own way. She'd been independent from an early age, accountable to no one, free to do as she pleased. Now she found she needed to learn what it was to be under authority – albeit the authority of a gentle but strong missionary she respected – and here the more placid Valerie proved a tremendous example.

Valerie benefited in other ways from the new arrival. She'd often felt a disappointment to Miss Dibden because of her unease about taking responsibility. Much as she loved the children, she was frankly scared of being left in charge and she knew, too, that she didn't command the kind of disciplined response from the children that Miss Dibden evoked. If a child needed a spanking it would be Miss Dibden who would mete out the punishment with the sole of her shoe applied to a bottom – a job which the tender-hearted Valerie found hard to do. But Wendy seemed positively to thrive on responsibility, and that took the pressure off Valerie.

Whether real or imagined, Valerie felt she was a disappointment to Miss Dibden over another matter, too: that of language learning. Struggle as she might, Valerie never seemed to make more than slow progress with her Cantonese, while Wendy, desperately keen to learn and more ready to plunge in headlong and "have a go", made the kind of progress that gave rise to an approving smile from Miss Dibden.

In spite of the austere surroundings – bare walls, high ceilings, rows of functional cots and tiered beds, few curtains and no carpets, four schoolrooms with desks in straight lines – it was a happy family. Yip, the Chinese surname taken for the family by Miss Dibden, means "fallen leaf". Many fallen leaves were grafted in, grew strong and blossomed.

Wendy's frequent letters and postcards home to her mother were bubbling and positive. In one, a few weeks after her arrival, she wrote of her planned first visit to Hong Kong Island for shopping. She seemed to be making the transition from earning a businesswoman's salary to counting the missionary pennies without too many regrets.

The world of "living by faith" was a new one for her. Those 76 hungry little mouths plus all the adult ones were kept well fed entirely by unsolicited donations. Miss Dibden presented every practical need to God and in faith expected Him to provide. He did – often in unexpected and incredible ways, through other Christians who were prompted to send gifts of money and through the generosity of local people. Funds and supplies, ranging from clothes and tins of milk powder to items of furniture and bundles of fresh vegetables, all arrived in response to prayer. As Wendy was to say later, "Miss Dibden was to me an amazing example of what it was to hear the Lord and obey and trust Him implicitly. Working with her was the best training ground I could have had."

Wendy's letter to her mother went on: "Yesterday it poured with rain as we arrived back at Shatin station from going to church in Kowloon. We were soaked, it really bucketed down. I must also get a light strong mac and some overboots. Today it is still raining. . ."

Wendy was getting acquainted with the propensity of the Hong Kong climate for sudden torrential downpours. But it was several months before the two women experienced their first typhoon, which turned out to be one of the worst in the territory's history.

TYPHOON WANDA

Typhoon Wanda in September 1962 was unusual in that the severe damage and loss of life were not caused by the wind or rain, but by a terrific tidal wave, and Shatin, basically a fishing settlement around an estuary, took its full force.

Radio warning was given of the approaching tidal wave. However, this was of little practical use to the majority of Shatin villagers. And an electricity cut early that morning deprived Miss Dibden and her family of the news. The Home, built sturdily on the small rocky hill, was little affected. But by the time the enormity of the disaster was appreciated it was too late for them to offer shelter to the nearby community.

At 9am every capable pair of hands at the Home was busy sweeping out the rainwater that battered its way in through the windows. Pausing on their brooms and peering through the gloom, Valerie and Wendy could see the fields of crops below were covered with water, which they attributed to the rain. But an hour later they were appalled to see that the level had risen some five feet up their hill, with many nearby shack homes completely lost to sight. On the few roofs still visible sat stunned villagers, clutching hastily assembled bundles of possessions and a few animals – pigs mostly, but also some chickens and dogs. The walled village to one side of the Home was well under water, and the Ecclesia Bible School by the bridge stood in grey water up to its windows.

Amazingly, by midday the water had retreated and the river inlet resumed its usual height. But the scene of devastation uncovered was heart-rending.

Miss Dibden, Valerie and Wendy ventured down the hill. The little narrow footbridge over the river had almost completely gone, as had whole shacks and even sections of brick-built homes. At the Bible School they found staff standing helplessly amid furniture and sodden books tossed and strewn everywhere. They heard how an *amah* had been rescued from near drowning in the basement.

Not everyone had been so fortunate. In the village they were told of a young baby being killed outright, crushed by one of the many metal pontoons unleashed by the tidal wave. Many villagers were missing, feared lost or trapped under the wreckage. People sat in the doorways of their ravaged shops, heads in hands. Windows gaped, doors hung drunkenly, tatters of clothing drooped feebly from fences and walls. Every yard of ground was littered with sorry debris of every kind, including the broken remnants of hundreds of lives – a child's toy car, a hairbrush with no handle, a cracked cup, an upturned wok, a wicker stool. Torn-up bushes and broken branches cluttered every path and a large fishing junk lay tossed inland some way, perched high on a heap of rubbish, lurching crazily to one side. It reminded Wendy of Noah's ark coming to rest on the peak of Mount Ararat.

The women found a pig, happily alive but exhausted, stranded in the lower limbs of a tree. Clambering through the mud and undergrowth, they released it, but saw dozens more animals lying lifeless everywhere.

The following day an inappropriate sun blazed down out of a clear blue sky as the three companions again walked through Shatin, where the rescue teams were now hard at work. It was a sobering scene – grim-faced workers laying out bodies in rows, while relatives squatted alongside loudly wailing, as was the local custom. Miss Dibden began to cry softly when she saw the naked body of a young child laid to rest on an old piece of cloth. The bloated, mud-caked bodies of pigs lying everywhere were already beginning to stink.

Farther on, the Army airstrip near the main road presented another chaotic scene. The back of the hangar was missing, and planes lay smashed like the playthings of some wilful child-giant. Cars had been somersaulted into ditches. Boats lay mauled – one even perched impossibly on the station railings. A dye works was a gutted shell, never to be re-opened. Several of the horses from the riding stables at Tai Wai were dead.

Clean water being in short supply, the amount of clearing up that could be tackled was limited, even for those with a heart to work. Some people were scavenging in the rubble, carrying off a few handfuls of sodden rice for a meal. But many just sat and stared, unseeing.

Men carrying sandbags were working where the sea wall, built just four years previously, had been invaded. Before Typhoon Wanda the wall had been lined with dozens of closely packed shacks, sometimes two deep, housing literally hundreds of families. Now only a few stray, hungry animals nosed the ground, wondering what had happened to their people and shelter.

The women felt guilty that their Home was so safe. A few broken windows and a couple of uprooted trees were the extent of the damage. When they later learned that the roof of the oldest part of the house had been damaged and needed replacing they felt almost relieved to be taking a small share of the hurt.

FOUR

Clouds – and a New Calling

The two young women were happily settled in Hong Kong, feeling fulfilled, loving the little Chinese orphans they worked with, learning much at the hands of Miss Dibden. What was there to disturb these satisfying days?

Two clouds appeared on the horizon. One, a faint and secret cirrus that at first hardly made an impact on the sunshine. The other more substantial, warning of a future storm.

The first resulted from Valerie and Wendy visiting a number of other children's homes, including the momentous few hours at Po Leung Kuk described at the outset of this book. These visits were prompted by a vague anxiety.

"Somehow we felt that our children didn't have enough home comforts. We knew that we were not to be critical of Miss Dibden and all she was lovingly providing for her family. It wasn't even reasonable to compare what she was doing with children's homes in the UK, where the situation and the government support were so vastly different. We decided to see around a number of children's homes in Hong Kong – that would be a fairer comparison," explains Wendy.

As their research progressed, they became aware of some devastating unmet needs, most dramatically evident in the lack of provision for Hong Kong's handicapped.

"In the early 60s Po Leung Kuk, funded by wealthy Buddhists with a concern for the community, and one wing of Tung Wah Hospital were really the only institutions offering places for mentally handicapped children," says Valerie.

She was the first to consider whether she herself might work with the handicapped. But neither she nor Wendy saw themselves as free to tackle the needs they saw and prayed for. They felt they had a commitment to Miss Dibden and they should be loyal to her until God showed them otherwise.

They were touched by the plight of these needy children and believed a loving Father God could meet those needs. However, if they envisaged their own involvement becoming a reality, they imagined it as some time in quite a distant future. They continued to pray that, if it was his will, God would make the way clear. So it was only an insignificant cloud in the sky.

Their two very different personalities were apparent in their reactions at this time of uncertainty. Valerie, in spite of her deep-rooted fear of responsibility, began quietly and calmly to accept what she increasingly believed to be a fresh calling from the Lord.

But Wendy was in the midst of a raging battle. "It was Aunty Donny who made me face up to things in the end. One evening we had supper with her and talked things over. She put her finger on my uncertainty right away. I could only mumble something non-committal when she challenged me."

Back in her room at Shatin that night Wendy was restless, feeling sure that she needed to be decisive. She was in a torment. "Was God calling us to work with the handicapped? Why couldn't I decide? I had gone over and over it all in my mind and searched myself.

"My biggest agony was fear that I wouldn't really be able to love handicapped children. I thought of the children we had visited, especially those at Po Leung Kuk. Some were so unattractive to look at, not beautiful at all. Some had unpleasant habits. Some had destructive, obsessional behaviour. How *could* I love them?

"Then there was the commitment. I was afraid to get

into something I wouldn't be able to get out of. Would I be trapped for the rest of my life?

"Finally, feeling broken by the struggle, I told God that I was *willing* to devote my life to working with the handicapped. *How* I could do it, I confessed to Him, I didn't know. But I was willing. And when I could say that to the Lord I experienced the most wonderful loving peace in my heart that I knew was from Him."

Changes in the minds and hearts of the two women were one thing. But their commitment to the Shatin Children's Home remained.

One day Miss Dibden, rather troubled, called Valerie and Wendy to her room. The second cloud was darkening her sky. She had been approached by the Social Welfare Department to allow her children to be adopted out of Hong Kong. A recent change in the law had allowed such adoptions and the demand had already taken all the eligible and available children from government institutions. But still families from overseas were writing, asking to adopt Chinese orphans.

The missionary's first reaction was to refuse. How could she lose all these children who meant so much to her? They were her family, her life, her love. Now she felt unsure. Had she made the right decision? She asked Valerie and Wendy to pray as she wrestled over it.

After some weeks Miss Dibden felt, not without much sadness, that she would be wrong to deny these youngsters the chance of a normal family life. But, she decided, she would release only the children aged 10 and younger. She believed the older ones would find it hard to settle into a family. She also insisted that, since her children had been brought up within the context of Christian teaching, they should go to the homes of practising Christians. Such was the high regard in which she was held, that her requests were granted. The processing and paperwork began.

Wherever possible the children's genetic families were

traced over the following months. There was an unhappy side to this. Four families who had abandoned babies now claimed back their children – and the authorities had no choice but to agree, even though it was recognised this probably meant that the families saw them only as sources of income. These children were now old enough to work in the markets or family businesses and earn a few dollars a week. There would be no more schooling for them. Many tears were shed over their departure.

But there were more positive prospects for the 25 children who went to families in New Zealand, for the 24 who went to the United States, and for the one little girl who was adopted by her "prayer aunty and uncle" in Ireland.

SUDDENLY FREE

With the Yip family so greatly reduced in numbers by the middle of 1963, Valerie and Wendy were now able to tell "Mama" of their concern for the handicapped and of their calling – and to receive her blessing.

They were free. Free to make real the vision of opening the home for handicapped children that now almost exclusively occupied their thoughts. But how to begin? Where? When? How would they fund such a project?

This last question was the most easily resolved. They would finance their work with prayer. Miss Dibden had introduced them to a prayer-answering God, a God who provided for real needs in response to faith. "Mama", they knew, had given them a most tremendous gift in allowing them that daily experience of dependence on God. It was a decision that made them excited, elated.

What should they call their work? That, too, was a question soon resolved. One day, travelling on the Star Ferry – one of the fleet of green and white double decker ferries that cross and re-cross the harbour for just a few cents a time – the two friends leaned over the rails discussing their plans and dreams.

Love, God's love in them to be shared with others, would be central to their work, they agreed. And so perhaps it should feature as part of their name. They began to talk of a favourite Bible verse from Lamentations: ". . . his compassions fail not. They are new every morning: great is thy faithfulness." They both loved the verse, and the great hymn based on it, written in the 1920s by Thomas Chisholm: "Great is Thy faithfulness, O God my Father."

By the time they reached the other side of the harbour, the name was chosen: The Home of Loving Faithfulness. God's love and God's faithfulness would be the foundation of their great adventure.

Training in love and faith they had already received in generous measure. But what about training to care practically for the handicapped? Formal qualifications requiring several years of training didn't seem appropriate, but they both felt the need for some specific short-term training.

In the meantime, their friend Joann Murray was increasingly involved in their discussions. Joann, a trained State Registered Nurse, had come to Hong Kong to work for a time with Archdeacon and Mrs Donnithorne. She began to get very excited about the plans for a home and tentatively talked about joining them. They all three agreed to make it a matter of prayer.

December 1963 saw Valerie and Wendy packing to return to England. They had both been accepted to do work experience at Queen Mary's Hospital in Carshalton, Surrey, though on what terms they weren't sure. Joann sailed for home, too, and by some happy "coincidence" got a job at the very same hospital.

MEANWHILE, BACK IN RUTLAND. . .
Wendy's mother had been following developments by mail. Not just from Wendy. Somehow, thinking of her own daughter being far from home and then thinking of Valerie as another young girl, but without a mother, Mrs Blackmur

had been including Valerie in the regular correspondence between Shatin and Rutland. She had begun to think of her as a second daughter. Through Wendy's lively letters she was also introduced to Joann and to many of the children at the Home. Wendy even sent her mother a tape of a day in the life of the Home.

Hearing that the Home was to be disbanded, with the children being adopted, Mrs Blackmur naturally anticipated a reunion. "When I heard the news, I thought Wendy would be coming back and started to make preparations. How wrong I was!"

Arriving home from work one evening, Mrs Blackmur found an airmail letter from Wendy waiting on the hall mat. As she usually did, she made a cup of tea and sat down to read it.

". . .So we shall be coming back to England by the end of the year. But don't think for one minute that we shall be staying. . ."

Only Mrs Blackmur's own words should describe what followed. "In between that sentence and the next one I became a Christian!

"When I sat down with my cup of tea and began to read that letter I was outside God's family. As I read that sentence I just stopped. 'God,' I said, 'I know I can't keep her. She's yours. She's given her life to you. And what's more, I want to give my life to you as well. You can do whatever you like with it'."

That same evening she wrote back to Wendy, telling her she had asked God to take her life. By return came a letter of encouragement from Wendy, and also a small black leather-covered *Daily Light* – a book of devotional Bible readings – inscribed "To second Mum, with much love and God's richest blessing, from Valerie".

39

FIVE

Training, Turmoil – and Homecoming

It was time for another divinely-appointed "nudge".

Valerie and Wendy had written to the Matron at Queen Mary's of their interest in the physically handicapped. As it turned out, those wards were fully staffed. But help, they were told on their arrival, was desperately needed with the severely retarded.

So they were assigned to two wards that cared for a total of 40 very helpless long-term patients under 16. By lunchtime on that first day when they met in the canteen to compare notes, they had both come to the conclusion that it was with these very children that their future lay. The Home of Loving Faithfulness would open its doors to the severely retarded, just as they felt their own hearts open in response to these they were now learning to work with. They both experienced an overwhelming love for the children.

So began 10 months of intensive on-the-job training as nursing auxiliaries, a period they began, by their own admission, as "totally green". Working on the wards and attending a short lecture course, they learned about the many and varied disabilities from which these children suffered: hydrocephalus, microcephalus, spina bifida, epilepsy, cerebral palsy, spasticity, chromosome disorders – an infinite variety of conditions resulting in differing degrees of mental handicap.

They learned about medication, physiotherapy and corrective surgery. Feeding, they found, was no simple matter, as many of the retarded had attendant physical abnormalities that confounded the normal processes of swallowing and digesting.

Even handling the children was a science. Twisted limbs put unusual strains on different muscles which had to be compensated for in lifting and bathing unless pain was to be caused. Positioning a child in bed so that a back twisted with scoliosis was properly supported was an art.

They learned much of the difficulties of parents through observation when families came to visit. They saw a whole spectrum of possible reactions – shame, embarrassment, impotency, disgust, ignorance, communication, compassion, sensitivity.

Valerie and Wendy were surprised to learn that they would actually earn a salary at Queen Mary's. It would enable them to save for the fares back to Hong Kong, they thought.

But within a week of working at the hospital came a further piece of good news. The Blue Funnel Line, knowing the nature of their recent trip back to England and the ambitions they held out for their return, wrote to offer them free passages to Hong Kong, valid for any May, June or July. They accepted immediately, booking their return for May of the following year.

Now, with the prospect of some unallocated salary plus some free months after the end of their hospital work experience, Valerie and Wendy did not need to think twice about how to spend both money and time.

They were attending Stanley Park Evangelical Free Church, conveniently situated near the back gates of the hospital. They asked the pastor if he could recommend somewhere offering short-term Bible training. His keen recommendation was for Capernwray Bible School in the Lake District, and so they – and Joann – quickly applied for the Winter Bible School which ran from October to March. Wendy, though, went through weeks of anxiety.

"I had the most awful time thinking that I would not be accepted. I was new to the faith. I wasn't spiritual enough.

Everyone would know so much more than me. I agonised over the testimony I had to write."

All three were accepted. Then Wendy faced another problem. Her grandfather died and she gave her mother all her savings to help pay for the funeral. The fees for each of the two terms were £39.

This second worry proved equally unnecessary. She received £25 from a Bible class she had spoken to; then a gift of £10 from the Stanley Park church; and anonymous best wishes in an envelope in her hospital pigeon hole were wrapped around a further £4. Wendy had always enjoyed accounts – but God's way of dealing with figures, how he could add up 25 and 10 and 4, was positively thrilling!

Lessons of faith over finance continued throughout their happy time at Capernwray. However, these faith-building experiences of provision faded into relative insignificance as Wendy faced her next problem. During the second term she went through a crisis about her calling.

Part of the Capernwray programme was to expose students to a variety of different international missions. And so it was that a young Norwegian girl came to speak of the work she was doing in Nepal. Suddenly Wendy was thrown into tremendous turmoil.

"I was under the most heavy conviction that I should go to Nepal to help this girl. Waking and sleeping I was haunted by those Nepalese faces I had seen on the slides, and I heard their voices calling out to me. How could I go ahead with the valedictory service being planned at the church in Stanley Park to send me out as a missionary to Hong Kong?"

And Valerie's reaction? "I felt shattered. How was I going to cope without Wendy? We were a team. I knew Wendy was going through a hard time – I could only pray."

One Sunday afternoon Wendy got to the point of writing to the pastor at Stanley Park, explaining her confusion and asking him to take her name off the details for the valedictory service. She signed it, sealed it in an envelope and went to Valerie's room. She couldn't bring herself to tell Valerie what the letter contained.

"I want to speak to Dr Stern. Do you think you could put this in the five o'clock mail collection if I'm not back by then?"

Dr J.C. "Charles" Stern, a visiting lecturer, listened hard as Wendy stumbled through the details of her bewilderment. His questions were simple and to the point.

"Did God call you to Hong Kong? Has He called you to work with handicapped children? Then he has not called you to Nepal."

The confusion vanished. "Immediately I knew he was right and immense peace flooded me. It was all so clear."

Wendy looked at her watch. Twenty past five. She raced off to Valerie's room.

But Valerie hadn't posted the letter. Afterwards she honestly couldn't remember Wendy giving her the letter at all, or why she should not have posted it. It didn't matter. Wendy was just thankful.

HOME TO HONG KONG

On 10th June, 1965, the Blue Funnel Line ship chugged gently into Hong Kong waters. Valerie and Wendy felt that they were coming home.

The previous few months seemed like a dream. That wonderful service at Stanley Park. The prayers and loving good wishes echoed in their hearts. And who would have thought that the Rev John Caiger of Gunnersbury Baptist Church would have agreed to give the message? When Valerie and Wendy had heard him pray at the Keswick Convention meetings the previous summer they had known that he was the man they wanted to speak at the valedictory service.

There was just one sadness. The service had been for two

of them, not three. After some heartsearching, Joann had decided to stay behind; it was hoped that she would join them later.

Valerie and Wendy thought contentedly of the large drums of equipment they had brought with them which somehow symbolised the realisation of their hopes and dreams. The drums were bursting with kitchenware, bedding, children's clothing and bales of towelling. During the sea journey they were able to have the use of a spare cabin and spent hours cutting and sewing ten sets of matching bath towels and flannels. Ten sets for ten children.

SIX

A Place with Potential

That June it rained hard every day. And every day they searched the newspaper columns.

At last one morning they saw an advertisement for a bungalow to let in Fan Ling, a few miles north of Shatin. The address was given as 59A On Lok Tsuen, with an asking price of $550 a month (£40 sterling or US$70 at 1991 exchange rates).

Wendy recalls: "We drove down a rough lane on the outskirts of Fan Ling. It was near a large Catholic school and some small factories. The house numbers didn't seem to be consecutive and we couldn't find the one we wanted. Then we spotted a bungalow being worked on – it was having a new brick wall built around it and was being redecorated. The number on the gatepost was almost totally obliterated. But it *could* have been 59A, so we went in to look around."

There was a pleasant garden with some hedges and a few trees including several firs and a lovely rose apple, and enough space for a car. The house was a concrete building in good condition, painted outside in brown and cream, with a front door leading off a verandah. Inside there was one large, long room with a neatly tiled floor. Two small, light rooms were to the right. And to the left a corridor led to two more living rooms, a small bathroom, an *amah*'s room with a cock loft, a kitchen and a back alley with a wall separating the house from the low slate roofs of a cluster of Chinese village houses.

"As soon as we walked in we could see its potential. As far as we could tell, there was just one drawback – we'd never be able to live with the newly-emulsioned bright, bright pink walls throughout!"

Actually there was another problem. This wasn't 59A. Much later they did eventually trace 59A, discovering a "poky little place with a bathroom no more than a bowl in a cupboard". No, this was in fact No 60 On Lok Tsuen. And the Chinese doctor who owned it was asking $900 (£67 or US$115) a month for it.

Valerie and Wendy had no doubts that God could give them that amount for the place of his choice – but they weren't sure it was really worth that much. And anyway, haggling was a time-honoured and respectable Chinese custom!

So, over a period of a month, and through the good offices of a young Chinese pastor who acted as intermediary, the negotiations went on, and were settled when the figure of $600 was agreed. The two women, though, felt certain they would become the new tenants long before the contract was signed, when they saw a workman painstakingly painting over all the lurid pink they had complained about!

The pastor acting as middleman didn't conclude the bargaining empty-handed. He was able to rent the smaller adjacent property, owned by the same doctor, to start up a kindergarten. And when Valerie and Wendy prayed for their first month's rent they also asked for – and received – enough to pay for the pastor's first $200 rent in thanks for his help.

Somehow the contents of the drums when unpacked and spread over the floor of their new home didn't seem to amount to very much. True, there were the two wooden bed bases locally made for $24 each, but the Chinese straw mats didn't do a lot to give them an impression of comfort. They had a restless first few nights. They had only one pillow, which Wendy insisted that Valerie should have, while she tossed about on an inflatable something which regularly deflated. After the silence of the Shatin hilltop it was disturbing to be so close to the medley of late night noise from the nearby homes – the clattering of mah jong tiles, the whining and barking of the wild and quarrelsome mangy dogs, the spitting of hot oil in blackened woks, the rumbling of the wheels of the hawker trolleys, the cackling of the wrinkled old women squatting to exchange coarse remarks from their doorways.

But things began to improve. A missionary friend arrived bearing gifts: two overlarge but wonderfully soft mattresses and some enormously long and sun-faded plum-coloured curtains – items being discarded by Kowloon's prestigious Peninsula Hotel. The curtains were amazing. After being soaked for several hours in a big zinc tub the dye ran, causing the bleached strips to totally disappear. Within days the whole house was curtained in beautiful pale plum, which admirably matched the now pale pink walls.

Other gifts and secondhand items arrived during those first few days: six cots; several elderly and very grimy dark green cupboards which were stripped down and repainted; a washing copper to use with the stone trough and standpipe in the yard which was their only means of washing clothes (the washing line was on the roof, reached by a metal staircase up from the kitchen); a spin-drier and a fridge; a stove bought for $50.

Valerie and Wendy also found they had inherited a ferocious-looking black dog from the previous caretaker of the bungalow. At first, terrified, they wouldn't approach him. But when no one came for him and he obviously needed feeding they overcame their apprehensions. After a while this abandoned creature became placid and affectionate. He was soon joined by three homeless kittens and a sick puppy. These were the first of dozens of sad and outcast animals who found shelter and care at the Home of Loving Faithfulness.

As soon as the bungalow began to have the semblance

of a home, Valerie and Wendy longed to take in their first children. In organising this they were given invaluable help by Miss S.C. Cheng, principle medical social worker at Queen Elizabeth Hospital. She visited the two young women regularly and introduced them to local medical and social workers. At a time when they had no telephone and no car she was tremendously valuable in helping them form useful contacts.

Miss Cheng, in her own words, "admired the courage, convictions and faith" of the two women and did all she could to offer encouragement. She helped them think through the criteria for admission and draft a form. Wendy, reflecting on how naive they were, considers that it was Miss Cheng's practical advice that enabled the Home to start on a sound footing.

It was Miss Cheng who warned that some people could be unscrupulous, drugging children to make them look more incapable so that they would be admitted on false pretences. She advised taking all children on trial for a month.

She also urged Valerie and Wendy to make a charge, however nominal, for each child. This advice also came from other quarters – but it was the one suggestion that they agreed together not to follow. They appreciated the thinking behind the idea of charging. Parents who paid, it was suggested, would value the place more and would have more reason to maintain a contact with the Home.

"But we felt quite clearly God saying 'Freely you have received, freely give'. So we decided to make no charge, a decision we never regretted. We also felt that parents tied to children by a monthly bill would become resentful."

Donations, generally quite small ones, continued to arrive and Wendy went to the bank at Fan Ling to open an account. In those days the accounts were still recorded on hand-written ledgers and Wendy was delighted to discover that the staff never wrote out the rather long name of the Home in full. Instead, they just penned a heart sign!

Another friend, senior radiologist Geoff Mauldon, advised the women they should get registered – something that had never occurred to them. And then Miss Cheng arranged for Valerie and Wendy to look at some of the children in need of placement attending the assessment clinic at Queen Elizabeth Hospital.

A POSTSCRIPT FOR MISS DIBDEN

The missionary lady who had been their teacher and inspiration left for England. With many of her children adopted out of Hong Kong, "Mama" took with her the remaining family of 22 Chinese daughters aged 11 to 13, not forgetting the gardener from the Shatin Home, Fa Wong, who had married one of her girls, Susan.

Friends helped buy Miss Dibden two adjacent houses in Portsmouth. As might be imagined, there was a lot of press coverage of the arrival of the unconventional family. Generally, they were well received and settled without fuss into the local secondary school, though in their late teenage years several of the girls developed identity problems and became obsessed with wanting to know about their Hong Kong backgrounds.

In spite of her long commitment to Hong Kong, Miss Dibden never afterwards yearned to return. Health-wise, England was far better for her, and she was able to recover from the attacks of malaria and sprue (a tropical disease of the intestine) to which she was subjected in Hong Kong. She was content to be a full-time mother to her girls and as they gained independence she would relax by painting watercolours of country scenes and flowers. At the Home of Loving Faithfulness the paintings of snowdrops in Valerie's room are her work. Sometimes she sold some of her paintings, sending the proceeds to the Home.

The courageous and pioneering work she had done

among Chinese orphans was never fully recognised in Hong Kong. But in England she was later awarded the MBE.

When all her girls had left, Miss Dibden moved into an old people's home in Tunbridge Wells. It was her wish not to be a burden to anyone as she got older. Many of her girls kept in touch, but a number of them caused her no small heartache. She died of cancer in December 1987, aged 82. Twenty three of her daughters attended the funeral service.

WAI SHEUNG
But to return to the Hong Kong of 1965. . .

Halfway up a steep hillside littered with huge boulders and latticed with evil-smelling streams, Valerie and Wendy located the mean hut. It was the usual haphazard construction of corrugated iron, sheets of rusty tin, broken pieces of plywood, cardboard boxes and bamboo poles which made it one of thousands that were a feature of the Hong Kong landscape of the 60s, especially in the New Territories. Even in the 90s the squatter hut is still to be found in remoter areas.

Not that the family living here owned this princely dwelling; they merely rented the back room. As was common in such a situation, there was no sanitation whatever. Water had to be carried up the rock-strewn hillside from a standpipe at the bottom, a walk of some 20 minutes.

Wai Sheung, aged three and a half years, was a tiny microcephalic, whose parents lived in abject poverty. By night she slept between her parents so that no harm could come to her, but she slept little and cried much. By day, for safety, she lay on a straw mat on the ground as the mother cooked and cared for the other children. Unavoidably, there she was attacked by ants and other insects, resulting in huge boils on her head.

A Place with Potential

WAI HONG

Wai Hong's parents lived in constant fear of eviction. Mother and father, three children and a blind grandmother all lived in a wooden cubicle about eight foot square. A small flat had been divided into nine such cubicles for renting out. Wai Hong, also a microcephalic, a long, thin, bright-eyed boy of five, had frequent bouts of flailing his limbs and banging on the thin wooden partitions, which caused complaints, cursing and threats from the neighbours. The parents, Muslims, cared well for him in these desperate circumstances. Father often spent all night up with him, holding tight his wild arms and legs and trying to calm him. Mother kept him scrupulously clean. They looked on the two women as something akin to miracle doctors, hardly daring to believe that anyone would want to help their little boy.

WING KIT

"Dah seh neh, dah seh neh" – those were the only words Wing Kit knew. They mean, "I'll kill you, I'll kill you!" When Valerie and Wendy heard him repeating the cruel phrase over and over, they knew the family's frustrations were boiling over in violence towards their youngest son. Two families shared the dark, stuffy and dirty room on one of the older resettlement estates at Shek Kip Mei. Wing Kit, a six-year-old with cerebral palsy and mental retardation, was an active little boy. But, the living conditions being what they were, he was kept in a few square feet behind a wooden fence just inside the door, which limited the damage when he threw himself around screaming, tearing his clothes and banging his head on the wall and floor. The family cooked on the verandah and a couple of times a day a bowl of rice was slid under the fence within his reach.

Wai Sheung, Wai Hong, Wing Kit. . . the first three arrivals, eagerly awaited by Valerie and Wendy, were brought to the Home of Loving Faithfulness on 13th August, 1965.

SEVEN

Early Battles

The joy of the two women was threatened within hours. Little Wai Sheung was fretful and miserable. As they held and tried to soothe her, she whimpered and tossed her head, now shaven and scarred following treatment for the boils.

Two days later, the child's mother arrived to see how she was settling in. When she saw Wai Sheung's obvious distress she produced a bottle of phenobarbitone from her bag, assuring Valerie and Wendy that she usually settled after a dose. When questioned previously, the mother had told them that Wai Sheung was receiving no medication – but in a way the news was quite a relief. It seemed likely that the child's behaviour was merely the result of being deprived of the drug.

However, by the evening Wai Sheung was running a fever. In spite of giving her a mild sleeping drug she slept not at all that night, and neither did her two anxious guardians. When morning light dawned they took her off to the nearby Lutheran Hospital in Fan Ling. Even as they waited to see a doctor the fever intensified and Wai Sheung began to have convulsions. The diagnosis was meningitis, evidently contracted before her arrival at the Home.

The following morning came the message to go immediately to the hospital. Wai Sheung was dead.

Shocked and silent, Valerie rushed off to the hospital. Leaving the bungalow, she bumped into Wai Sheung's mother. Taking her arm, she steered her towards the hospital, trying to prepare her for news of her daughter's death. Wendy stayed to care for their two little boys, Wai Hong and Wing Kit, fighting back tears as she poured out her feelings to God.

"Why, God, why? Why have you allowed Satan to do this to an innocent little child? Why have you allowed our work to be destroyed before we've even begun?"

Valerie, anticipating the usual Chinese custom of loud wailing and weeping for the dead, was relieved that the mother was surprisingly calm. "I remember that what upset her most was that her daughter had such a short time to enjoy the lovely white painted cot we had prepared for her."

Over the next few days that empty white cot remained a rebuke to their faith, their competence, their calling.

"But God seemed to be telling us to hold on to what was true," recalls Wendy. "And what was true was that he himself had called us to this work."

A BATTLE OVER A BOTTLE

The defeat Valerie and Wendy felt over the death of Wai Sheung threatened to multiply as they battled hourly with one of the boys.

Wai Hong, or Fu Fu to call him by the pet name by which he soon became known, was quite simply addicted to the bottle and to his mother. She had laboriously bottle-fed him for all his five and a half years. Very concerned, she had spelled out the problem to Valerie and Wendy. If anyone else tried to feed him, or if she tried anything but a bottle, he would scream.

And scream he did – loud and long. There was battle royal three times a day as they tried every imaginable method of feeding him. He would only scream and vomit.

Fu Fu's mother came to visit. Smiling, she told Valerie and Wendy that they had worked wonders. Her son wouldn't take a bottle from her – surely that meant he must be full and happy! The two friends returned her smiles nervously, and said nothing. Inwardly they were full of fear.

They worried: "One child has died, a second refuses

to feed. What if his mother takes him away? People will say we can't cope and then Wing Kit will be taken away, too."

For nine long days Fu Fu screamed at every attempt to feed him. Valerie and Wendy were at the end of their imagination, patience and resources.

"That ninth evening we realised we had been trying in our own strength to solve Fu Fu's feeding problem. We felt led to cast our burden upon the Lord and for the first time prayed in faith, really believing that God himself would undertake."

The next morning they supported Fu Fu's flaccid body yet again in the little rattan chair and Wendy raised the spoon to his mouth. He took it "like a little lamb"! It was a significant and wonderful breakthrough. The next day when his mother visited she found Fu Fu happily eating milled food from a spoon — something she'd been unable to achieve. She was so amazed she rushed back home to fetch the father, so that he could see it.

After an unpromising start, Fu Fu gained weight. Given ample space to spread his unruly limbs, he gradually grew less violent in his movements. And 26 years later he's a lanky lad with a stubbly chin who's loved by many.

NEVER A MOMENT'S TROUBLE

If Wing Kit could learn to say "Dah seh neh — I'll kill you", Valerie and Wendy had hopes that he could forget that and learn new things. He did forget those words. But, amazingly, even decades of loving care later, if an arm is raised near him he flinches — such is the power of the memory of his early beatings. It was, though, a thrilling moment when Wing Kit said very clearly one Christmas Day, "Jesus! Birthday!"

He was more mobile than Fu Fu, able to sit unaided and bounce around. From the first day, "he never gave a moment's trouble — apart from his habit of stripping off his clothes whenever the opportunity arose!" In time, although dragging one weaker leg, he learned to walk.

ANDREW'S STORY – PART 1

Mr Sung, a taxi driver, had a difficult life. His wife had left him and the four children a year before. The oldest, a daughter, was only 10. The two youngest of his three sons were mentally retarded.

As in most Chinese communities, the neighbours in Mong Kok tried to help. But many were elderly and couldn't cope well, especially with little Kin Nin. At two years old, he was obviously going to be even more retarded than his five-year-old brother. He was as helpless as a newborn, with no head control, no strength in his spine, and no indication that he would ever speak, feed himself or become toilet trained.

Valerie and Wendy met Mr Sung when he took his two sons for assessment at the hospital clinic. He went down on his knees in desperation, pleading with them to take the boys.

With only ten places to fill and two now taken, Valerie and Wendy decided it wouldn't be right to take two children from one family. The five-year-old, although mentally inadequate, could walk with the aid of calipers and was not too difficult to care for. Indeed, eventually this boy was able to attend a special school. But Kin Nin they would take. He became part of the Home of Loving Faithfulness family in September, 1965.

It soon became apparent that Kin Nin's disabilities were more linked to malnutrition and neglect than mental deficiency. He was diagnosed as severely retarded, but it was obvious to Valerie and Wendy that his bright eyes betrayed a level of observation that happily mismatched the clinical report.

He was a demanding child. If one of them left the room he would scream and exhibit classic temper tantrum traits.

Valerie and Wendy rightly deduced that this behaviour was more the result of total insecurity and psychological damage caused by a lack of love than the symptoms of brain damage.

He had a great deal of potential. They set to work at once to extend his limited horizons. A session with a speech therapist confirmed that his lack of speech was due to emotional problems. Very slowly, the long and violent screaming fits gave way to attempts to babble a few sounds.

"That first year with us he made terrific development – walking, becoming toilet trained, feeding himself," Wendy remembers.

His progress was wonderful in the eyes of both women. But its very success created problems. Surely he was now inappropriately placed with the severely retarded? With love and encouragement perhaps Kin Nin would be able to contribute to the wider world.

They approached the Evangel Children's Home, which cared for 27 children in a warm, family atmosphere, and with his father's permission the three-year-old was transferred there in September, 1966.

That might well have been the end of Kin Nin's story as far as the Home of Loving Faithfulness was concerned. But things worked out differently, so that Kin Nin – or Andrew, as he was to become – is still today as much a member of the family as Fu Fu and Wing Kit are, though in quite another way.

Valerie and Wendy, deciding it would be disturbing to visit little Kin Nin at the Evangel Home, phoned frequently to ask about his progress. By that first Christmas all was not well.

"Regretfully, his psychological and emotional needs were not really being met. The staff had lots of problems with him – so many that the housemother was threatening to leave," says Wendy.

It became an issue of either Kin Nin or the housemother, and in February the boy returned to the bungalow in Fan Ling.

"It was a step backwards – but passing him around from place to place was not going to help him. We did contact the father and asked if he would consider taking him back now that there was so much improvement in his capabilities. But father had remarried and there was a new baby – and the wife threatened to walk out if Kin Nin came back."

By this time Wendy and Valerie had, of course, taken in more children, so they had less time to give to the little boy. They needed to find a way to provide Kin Nin with the stimulus he needed for progress. At first he attended the Chinese kindergarten next door, but it was too easy for him to slip out of class and run home. He was transferred to another kindergarten in nearby Sheung Shui, and this worked well for some time, but problems came when he needed help with homework. Already at a major disadvantage academically alongside "normal" children, Kin Nin struggled with his Chinese. The local education system seemed likely to prove too demanding for him. Perhaps English would be easier? Valerie and Wendy turned their attention to the English medium schools. At the age of six he was accepted at a school on a nearby British Army base, where he did well.

Then an English family they knew became interested in adopting Kin Nin. He began to spend weekends with them – and it was they who named him Andrew. The slow processing for adoption began. It was a blow when the wife failed the routine medical examination. Previously she had suffered a nervous breakdown while the family were in Nepal, and the diagnosis was that some instability remained.

Undeterred, Valerie and Wendy began to work through the system again when some New Zealand relatives of a local missionary expressed a desire to adopt Andrew. It seemed an ideal situation – a family with four children, living on a farm. They envisaged the boy growing in strength and stamina and enjoying the outdoor life.

The wheels of bureaucracy trundled slowly. Almost a year passed from the initial interest, by which time the family's situation had drastically altered. The wife had developed a serious illness and they were forced to sell the farm. They withdrew from the adoption.

Perhaps it was hardly surprising that Andrew's school career was now not proceeding well. His behaviour was disturbed and Valerie and Wendy were asked to remove him from the Army school.

Rejection. . . hope. . . rejection. . . hope. Was this to be the continuing pattern of Andrew's life?

Andrew's story really *does* have the happiest of endings, and our account will return to him. But in the meantime much was happening in the lives of Valerie and Wendy, and other children had made their debut on the scene.

By the time they celebrated their first Christmas in the bungalow at Fan Ling, the Home of Loving Faithfulness family had grown to eight. To their three boys – Fu Fu, Wing Kit and Kin Nin – were added five girls – Siu Kuen, Ngan Ying, Shaan Shaan, Laan Chan and Siu Fong.

EIGHT

Three More Children

Like Andrew's father, Siu Kuen's father drove one of the hundreds of red and grey taxis that are a convenient and cheap method of travel in Hong Kong. Mr and Mrs Wong were cousins, which may explain why the first two of their three children were severely mentally retarded. The family lived in a hut near the railway line at Kowloon Tong, the mother working when she could as an *amah* for a western family.

As before, Valerie and Wendy decided to take the child which was the greatest burden to the family.

Four-year-old Siu Kuen was microcephalic, like Fu Fu, but also very spastic, with rigid limbs, her legs naturally "frogged" outwards and her arms perpetually raised. As if in compensation, she was blessed with a gorgeous smile and surprisingly curly black hair.

She settled into the Home with difficulty, crying often for attention – which she responded to with giggles, loving to be with people. Her spasticity made her difficult to handle and a special rattan chair with a tray was made in which to sit her up occasionally, otherwise she was always laid on her back.

Because they felt Siu Kuen needed so much prayer, Wendy wrote to her mother in England to ask her to become the little girl's "prayer aunty". Mrs Blackmur faithfully prayed for Siu Kuen until the girl died peacefully of bronchiectasis after a long illness in October 1984, over 19 years after her admission. By then both of Siu Kuen's parents and two younger, normal, children had emigrated to the United States. But, a touching postscript, a young teenage cousin visited her in hospital and stayed with her for hours during her last few days. This lovely girl, Alice, was still in touch with the Home years later.

NGAN YING

When nine-year-old Ngan Ying arrived in October that first year, she was carried to the Home on her grand-mother's back. Ngan Ying had been born a normal healthy baby, but at a few months old had developed meningitis, which led to hydrocephalus, a condition once known as "water on the brain". The hydrocephalus had sponta-neously arrested, but not until spinal fluid had caused the atrophy of many brain cells. So Ngan Ying was retarded, her head over-large, her body and limbs small and thin.

But from the beginning she was a child who earned a reputation for her bright, mischievous, lovely personality, and became known for her smiles and giggles. Her great sense of humour found expression in dozens of naughty little tricks such as making holes in her mosquito net. But she never cried, seemed to understand much, and appeared to appreciate the care she was given.

Amazingly, after several months at the Home, Ngan Ying began to speak. Wendy remembers how it began.

"Her bed was by a window overlooking the garden. I used to call our old black dog over to his food. One day I heard Ngan Ying calling, just like I did, 'gow, gow, gow' – the Cantonese for 'dog'. Next we noticed she was perfectly imitating the few sounds that Fu Fu made. He used to say 'golly, golly, golly', to which she would add 'oh gear', for 'oh dear'. We encouraged her and she began saying quite a few words in both English and Cantonese. She couldn't say some sounds, such as 't' and 'd'. She used to call me 'Angy Wengy'.

"Her grandma loved her and used to visit her a lot, but the parents rarely. We asked them if Ngan Ying had ever spoken at home. She hadn't. The mother said she'd never bothered to speak to her because the doctor had told them she would never understand anything.

"Soon she was talking a lot, and her repertoire included some words she must have remembered from before coming to us, which seemed incredible. For example, we never allowed anyone to smoke in the Home, but one day she picked up the thin cardboard tube from inside a reel of cotton that I had thrown into her cot for her to play with. She stuck it into her mouth and began to playact smoking, holding her fingers just right. 'What are you doing, Ngan Ying?' I asked her. 'Sik ling gai,' she replied – 'Smoking'. We checked and found that indeed grandma did smoke."

Later, Valerie and Wendy moved her bed so that she was facing the kindergarten playground next door. Immediately Ngan Ying set herself to learn all the tunes and words of the nursery rhymes she could hear. Eventually they could count 100 songs that she knew, albeit some with rather indistinct words. Ngan Ying was not the only one delighted with her achievement.

Eventually she became wonderful company, could hold a reasonable conversation, and was very sociable – sometimes until three o'clock in the morning! She could tease the staff, make simple jokes, and astonish callers by picking up the telephone and saying 'wai' – 'hello'.

Sadly, as Ngan Ying's years increased so did the frequency of her fits. Aged 17, she was admitted to hospital with uncontrollable convulsions. Taken in at 83 pounds, she returned three weeks later weighing just 50 pounds, and robbed of many of her hard-won and much-enjoyed abilities. Her sight had gone, though later she regained some peripheral vision upwards. Her thin limbs were very contracted. She never spoke again, although, being Ngan Ying, she tried so hard. For the next three years she had to be tube-fed, since swallowing caused incessant coughing. Later, slow and tortuous spoon feeding became possible.

Still at times she laughed and giggled. She was in every

way – and remains to this day – the model patient, in spite of deteriorating health and increasing pain as she battles with bronchiectasis and skin complaints.

SHAAN SHAAN

The very thought of this pretty and responsive little girl being sent to the Po Leung Kuk children's home made Valerie and Wendy shudder.

Shaan Shaan, very spastic, had been abandoned at a few days old and had been brought up in a children's home – in fact the first home that Miss Dibden had founded, which was afterwards run by an American charity. Now Shaan Shaan was five years old and her future was uncertain. She neither fitted in with the babies group at the home nor with the normal children her age. Po Leung Kuk was the only option, if the Home of Loving Faithfulness could not give her a place.

Valerie and Wendy had agreed that they wouldn't take children from other institutions as their priority would be to relieve needy families of the pressures of coping with a severely handicapped child. But, with that threat hanging over the little dark head, they couldn't turn their backs on her. Shaan Shaan became a lively and lovable member of their increasingly hectic Fan Ling household.

She was from the first a determined young lady. She was never able to speak but communicated volumes with her eyes, leaving no one in doubt of her feelings and responses. She always understood a great deal and loved to be in on a joke. And from the beginning she was aware of the other children in a positive way.

"I would walk her round to every cot and say 'Good night' to everyone. She would put a hand on each one. Sometimes we would tell her needs for prayer and she would clasp her hands together," says Wendy.

Is it really possible for children such as Shaan Shaan to have an awareness of God? Yes indeed – and more. Valerie and Wendy believe that there is a plane of spiritual contact experienced by handicapped children that is denied to those of "sounder" mind.

Valerie explains: "Because we love the Lord we are ministering to them in His name. We love them to listen to Christian songs or Bible readings. When I say 'Good night' to the children, I always tell them that I love them and that God loves and protects them. I believe it's important to talk to them about Jesus and certainly the more able children understand that Jesus loves them. In fact, all kinds of talking to the children is important. Even if they don't understand the words, your tone of voice can convey so much.

"If a child doesn't have the brain capacity to understand about sin then he or she is the Lord's anyway. I think these children can be in communion with God more than we are."

Wendy, too, believes that the child with a severely damaged mind and body has a spirit that is unaffected by handicap.

"I believe that these children's relationships with God are so much freer than ours. They are not hindered by the temptations and sins that spoil our relationships with God. We see such trust and rest in the children, even though they can't explain it.

"Children that never reach an age of discretion mentally are never accountable to God in the same way that we are. They will all go to Heaven."

Some of the abler children, particularly those with Downs syndrome, can, they are sure, come to a saving "knowledge" of Jesus Christ.

"One of our children, Chan Mei, for example, has definitely acknowledged that she needs Jesus to wash away her sin," says Wendy.

"Of the others, some, like Shaan Shaan, understand the concept of prayer. There is a way in which she can pray that we are never able to understand. When we ask her to pray about something, she puts her hands together but never makes a sound."

Wendy has a vivid memory of another child, Fung Tai, being in a prayer meeting with them and suddenly launching into a stream of fluent communication that was in no language any of them knew. They were all convinced that she was using the spiritual gift of tongues.

But back to Shaan Shaan's story. She was always feminine, loving pretty clothes and definite about which colours she liked to wear. Although not keen on soft toys or dolls, she loved musical or mechanical toys tied onto her cot and could manipulate them with her toes if the winders or pull strings were large enough. As a six- and seven-year-old she could wriggle herself around the floor of the Home, head first, and loved being given little chores. After tea every day she had the task of manoevring the socks off all the children and dropping them into a bowl for washing.

During her teenage years Shaan Shaan could be very moody, and Valerie and Wendy had to be careful not to tease her. She went through a period of hypersensitivity. Too much sympathy from others when she wasn't feeling too good would result in floods of self-pitying tears.

Generally, Shaan Shaan's health was good. But in 1982 she suddenly developed symptoms of stomach obstruction. Surgeons discovered a tight band of muscle in the abdomen.

The road to recovery was slow. Shaan Shaan lost a great deal of weight and looked gaunt and ill – and she knew it. A plan was devised to restore her determination. Her hair was permed, her face flattered with cheerful make-up, her nails brightened with varnish. Valerie and Wendy pushed her into the playroom in a wheelchair, positioning her next to a large mirror. Shaan Shaan spent the day there, with a constant stream of visitors just "happening" to drop by.

"Shaan Shaan, you look gorgeous with your hair like that!"

"What a super outfit. You look great!"

"You really are looking fit and well today!"

It worked! Shaan Shaan blossomed again from that day.

One of Shaan Shaan's greatest joys in the 26 years she has been at the Home of Loving Faithfulness is the special relationship she has with her "prayer aunt". Nesbit Ferguson, from Scotland, who had been a supporter of Miss Dibden's work, asked to be involved in the new work and "adopted" Shaan Shaan. Though now a lady in her 60s, Aunt Nesbit still sends gifts, letters and postcards to her special "niece".

In 1988 Shaan Shaan's stomach obstruction problems recurred. She became extremely ill and several weeks after surgery was sent home from hospital just before Christmas, not expected to live. All who knew and loved her grieved to see the yellow waxen skin stretched over a frail, bony frame.

"Nursing her the first day she was home from hospital we knew that only a miracle could save her. It was Christmas-time, and we were short-staffed, so we made the awful decision to get her coffin made by our handyman Kim before he took some days off. We really expected her to die over the holiday."

Amazingly she survived Christmas. They began to hope a little. Through early January she made minimal progress, hardly tangible. At her darkest hour she weighed just 44 pounds but by the beginning of February she had, unbelievably, crept up to 55 pounds. Then, during a time of crisis with another child dying in hospital, she suddenly had a relapse, returning to 47 pounds. Her eyes told of the agony she was suffering. The prayers continued.

"Shaan Shaan, you can make it! A promise – if you can reach 60 pounds we'll take you. . . to the ballet!"

The ballet! Shaan Shaan loved the ballet. She had been

taken several times before and it was her favourite treat.

Slowly, so slowly, with love and encouragement, Shaan Shaan's will to live rose, her body strengthened, the deathly pallor faded.

By April she had reached 59 pounds and the scales hovered there for three weeks. They couldn't risk her regressing. "Hope deferred makes the heart sick," Proverbs says. The much talked-of trip to the ballet was arranged.

May 1989 in Hong Kong. It was the time of the pro-democracy marches in the city, as thousands identified with the student protesters over the border in Beijing. It was that time of high hopes and euphoria that preceded the horror of the 4th June massacre in Tiananmen Square.

The students were out on the streets; there were banners unfurled and voices raised. Wendy felt one with them in spirit, as she drove through the crowds to get to the Academy of Performing Arts. But she had an additional reason for her hope - the excitement in Shaan Shaan's eyes.

Shaan Shaan's recovery from the very brink of death was nothing short of a miracle. Apart from an increase in the tight angling of one arm, there was soon little to remind anyone of the skeletal features she had worn for many months. Colour returned to her cheeks and vivacity to her determined spirit. In the summer of the following year, she made Hong Kong history as well as a number of personal "firsts". The Government departments had never before issued an I.D. card and a passport to a mentally handicapped adult with no known surname. A delighted, giggling and shrieking Shaan Shaan, escorted by Wendy and her mother, went on the adventure holiday of a lifetime, flying to Singapore to stay with supporters of the Home.

NINE

And Two More Makes Eight

Many proud skyscrapers dominate the Hong Kong sky-line. But thousands of rooftops of meaner dwellings are crowded with illegal constructions of wood, bamboo and corrugated iron which house some of the city's most desperately poor.

LAAN CHAN

Laan Chan's family lived in such a rooftop home in Mong Kok, reached by a filthy, dark stairway with no rails. The rough shack, composed of pieces of reject timber, scrap aluminium and dirty sacking, had no electricity and no water supply. Ten-year-old Laan Chan, post-meningitis epileptic and retarded, lived in a world of her own. Brain damage had taken from her the use of the right side of her body. She arrived at the Home, "a grubby, sleepy child", not long before their first Christmas.

Laan Chan is one of those retarded children who, to all appearances, knows nothing and no one and, as Valerie says, could easily be dismissed as "a bit of a blob". But those that care for her suspect a whole reservoir of untapped intelligence.

At one time Laan Chan was discovered to be conducting a campaign of terror against Shaan Shaan, bringing her heel down hard on the other girl's face as the children were lying on mats on the verandah in the afternoon sunshine. The attacks were carried out secretly when Laan Chan thought she was unobserved, and she would always stop abruptly when her name was called.

"From then on we knew that not only did she know her name, but she knew right from wrong. A brain scan later revealed that at frequent intervals she had as much as seven seconds of normal brain activity. The doctor said that had she been given correct training at an early age she could have been much more responsive than she is."

SUSIE

Little Siu Fong – always known as Susie – also came into the Home that first year. Aged three, she was epileptic, microcephalic, and blind, multiple handicaps caused by a rare condition only diagnosed after a further three years as Incontinentia Pigmenti. The illness is characterised by extensive brown blotching of the skin.

The case was referred to them by the Save the Children Fund organisation. Susie's mother, desperately poor, lived in a resettlement flat at Tsuen Wan. The father was a deckhand, away at sea for long stretches of time. Two daughters born before Susie had both died of the same condition, which is apparently passed on from mother to daughters.

Susie's chronic epilepsy made for stressful nursing.

"I remember the first time she had a status epilepticus – continuous convulsions as opposed to petit or grand mal fits," recalls Wendy.

"After about an hour we decided to take her to the clinic. It was night time, so I strapped her into the front seat of the car, fixing a torch onto the glove compartment shining into her face so that I could watch what was happening as I drove. I shook all the way there, expecting her to cyanose and die. But she recovered – and we learned to cope with these attacks.

"By observation we found her terrible fits often started with her giving a loud shout and then she would hold her breath or give soundless cries. We often threw iced water on her to make her gasp for air."

Susie needed anti-convulsants three times daily. But she hated the taste and refused to take the food in which the pills were disguised. Some days all that she would take was three ounces of glucose, painfully slowly, by spoon.

Wendy loved the little girl dearly – and often found herself desperate. "I got uptight about Susie's feeding and would shout to God to do something. In the end I would even get angry with her. Every mealtime she would cry and scream. It was terrible. I always ended up in tears.

"One day in frustration I threw her onto my bed, which fortunately had a thick mattress. When I realised what I'd done, I just broke down beside her. But with this incident God got through to me. I knew I was never going to feed her by my will. I began to ask God to be the drugs and food to her that she couldn't take. Then I was able to relax with her, even when she refused to feed."

However, Susie continued to lose weight. Talking with a hospital specialist, it was thought that maybe a period of being fed by tube would break through the psychological barrier she had erected.

After three weeks in hospital, Susie was obviously hating it there, and it was heartbreaking for the women to visit her and leave her crying. The ward doctor began to speculate that she'd lost her swallowing reflex and Valerie and Wendy feared a long stay away from home.

Wendy had a rare day off and couldn't get Susie out of her mind. Perhaps she would be allowed to take her out for an hour's drive. She would get her back to the ward by eleven o'clock and still have the rest of the day for the shopping and dressmaking she'd been planning for weeks.

With the doctor's permission Wendy got Susie dressed. One of the ward sisters hovered around the foot of the bed. "Of course, children like this. . . well, it's not fair on anyone, is it? Children like this would be better off if they were never allowed to live at all. I mean, what's the use. . ."

Wendy was angry. "In God's sight this little girl is as valuable as you are. . ."

The sister dismissed her with a wave of the hand. "Here,

take a feeding bottle. And have her back by five o'clock."
She strode off.

"Five o'clock? I'll have her back by eleven." Wendy's
words were lost to the starched back already half way
down the ward.

By the time Wendy had reached the YMCA in Salisbury
Road, Kowloon, she was, in her own words, "convicted
about my own selfishness".

In those days the YMCA's rooftop cafeteria was one of
her favourite places – alas, demolished in 1989 to make
way for bigger and better. It was a modest, quiet place
where you could buy a simple snack quite cheaply and
enjoy a magnificent view of the harbour.

Ignoring the stares, she sat the little girl on her lap
and ordered warm milk and cake. She soaked the cake
in the milk and put it to Susie's lips. Susie refused it,
but eventually allowed some milk to be dribbled into her
mouth. Then Wendy bought some chocolate drops, which
Susie began to eat.

"I sat there, watching the clock, having an argument
with the Lord. I had so much planned for my precious
day off. But in the end I spent the whole wonderful day
with her."

With Susie in her arms, Wendy crossed the harbour on
the Star Ferry and, oblivious to the hoards of tourists
open-mouthed at seeing such a very handicapped child
on an outing, boarded the Peak Tram. They rode to the
top – the famous Victoria Peak. From here, mist and smog
permitting, it's possible to duplicate the Hong Kong view
of so many picture postcards.

"There was a playground there, a little out of the way
of the shops and restaurants thronging with tourists. I sat
swinging with her on my lap, singing to her in my croaky
old voice and feeding her chocolate drops. She ate the
whole packet. She was so happy and relaxed and so was
I. Who cared about the shopping and dressmaking?"

Promptly at five o'clock Wendy returned the little girl to the hospital. The next day the doctor called to say Susie could be discharged; she was eating and drinking normally.

Wendy could hardly believe what God had done.

"I'd wanted to be so selfish. I wanted that day off and at the beginning was so resentful of spending any more than an hour with Susie. But, in exchange, God had given me – and Susie – so much."

JOINED BY JOANN

The family was growing. As well as having eight children by that first Christmas, 1965, Valerie and Wendy had been joined by Joann from England and their first Chinese *amah*, Ah Jing.

Joann had been struggling with some hesitations about joining Valerie and Wendy, and a not insignificant amount of pressure from her family, who advised her that she would be throwing her life away in Hong Kong. Somehow, Joann brought her doubts with her. And living and working in an increasingly cramped space at Fan Ling put all three of them under pressure. Perhaps it wasn't surprising that differences in character began to manifest themselves in tension and arguments. Valerie and Wendy screened themselves from much of the stress by their shared sense of humour. But Joann was more serious by nature, and attempts to bridge the gap between them often failed. It was some time before she admitted that the "fooling around" of the other two actually upset her. She was a very caring person, but worked slowly, and the quick routines already established between Valerie and Wendy made her feel insecure.

It soon became obvious that two plus one might never become three. Christmas was cold in ways that extra blankets couldn't cover. Inevitably, Valerie and Wendy voiced their criticisms of Joann together and resentments grew on both sides.

Then the situation changed radically. Valerie went into hospital with a slipped disc and Joann left her language study to help Wendy. Wendy, at first rebelling at the thought of working closely with Joann, discovered that, amazingly, they got on very well together. When Valerie returned she found a situation in which she, and not Joann, felt the outsider – to which she reacted by withdrawing into herself.

It was the first relationship crisis of the fledgling work – and it was not to be the last. It was resolved neither quickly nor neatly. Valerie was introverted and isolated for months and the rift between her and Wendy grew. Wendy recalls one frightening evening when Valerie was missing for hours.

"Jo and I were so scared. Finally I heard Valerie come in and I pretended to be asleep because I didn't know how to react to her. Then I heard a noise and realised she was moving her mattress out of our room into the kitchen. It was one of the rare times I saw her cry. She felt unwanted. I took the mattress back in and we both sat on the bed, feeling helpless."

Valerie cried out to Wendy, "Pray that I will be released from the devil's hold on me!"

In the moments that followed her distress tangibly lessened. "As Wendy prayed such a feeling of peace and cleansing came to me. The next morning I was able to ask Joann to forgive me, and that was the beginning of healing in our relationships."

The strains of the threesome were further relieved by the arrival of a fourth young woman. Irene, a gentle, quiet trained nurse in her early twenties, was a contact from their Queen Mary's days who had become a Christian through Joann's witness. She joined them in May 1966 and shared a flat in Kowloon with Joann, the two of them attending language study together. Joann had a genuine desire to meet local people and share the Christian Gospel so it seemed sensible to release her for language study. A routine was established – Joann and Irene worked at the Home two weekends each month, allowing Valerie and Wendy some much-needed time off from their demanding family.

However, Irene's heart had been lost from the work before she had set foot in Hong Kong. On the voyage she had met and fallen in love with one of the ship's officers, a Singaporean called Noel. Their wedding took place about a year later at the Mariners' Club in Kowloon. Soon afterwards, by amicable agreement, Joann left, too, the final decision precipitated by her need for an operation for a detached retina.

Valerie and Wendy were more grateful than ever for the help of Ah Jing, their first local Chinese helper. Aged just 15 when she came, she was paid $90 a month (about £7 sterling or US$11 at 1991 exchange rates). She became far more than an *amah*, progressing from domestic work, shopping at the market and cooking to learning to feed and care for the children.

TEN

And Two Teenagers Make Ten

Valerie and Wendy had set themselves the goal of having ten children at the Fan Ling bungalow. This they achieved within twelve months of their arrival. By August of 1966, to their three boys – Wing Kit (7), Fu Fu (6), and Andrew (3) – and five girls – Laan Chan (11), Ngan Ying (9), Siu Kuen (5), Shaan Shaan (5), and Susie (4) – they added two teenage girls, Fung Tai and Chan Mei.

FUNG TAI
Fung Tai, stated the referral report, was helpless as a result of cerebral palsy and epilepsy. She lived with her mother in a stone hut in one of the remoter New Territories villages. Mother sold vegetables at the market, which meant leaving Fung Tai alone from very early in the morning.

Valerie's visit to the girl, admitted to a hospital ward following a status epilepticus, confirmed Fung Tai's needy condition. The child looked distant, pathetic and physically incapable.

The 14-year-old's arrival at the Home of Loving Faithfulness, though, presented a very different picture.

As soon as she was lifted off her mother's back and deposited on the floor, Fung Tai scooted along on her bottom, picked up a copy of a Reader's Digest upside down and gabbled on excitedly, pretending to read. An astounded Valerie could hardly believe this was the same girl she had visited. They could only assume that Fung Tai had previously been heavily sedated. However, from the day she arrived, Fung Tai behaved as if she had been with them always, and her staying with them was never questioned.

She couldn't walk, but shuffled with dexterity on her bottom. Chairs and wheelchairs were tried without success, for Fung Tai was never really at ease unless she was at ground level. Eventually a compromise was reached: a specially made skateboard upon which she was happily mobile. She had never worn shoes on her rounded feet. After much searching in the markets the only footwear at all possible proved to be cheap white plimsolls. But, as Wendy recalls, "You would have thought they were Cinderella's glass slippers, so delighted was she with them!" Fung Tai loved her new clothes and shoes and loved going out to show them off. She spoke, albeit incoherently, some Hakka and some Cantonese words, and gradually she learned some English. In the early days Fung Tai's mother did visit, but stayed just a few minutes and later came not at all. Fung Tai talked a lot about her mother and it was hard to know how to reply. Socially outgoing, she loved all visitors and would admire their shoes, bags, beads or other accessories – and not infrequently visitors would leave minus one or two items they had surrendered to her!

Fung Tai's teenage years were marked by a series of "crushes" on different people. She adored Joann. Later, her devotion was directed at another staff member, Janet. Her next love was an elderly cook, Ah Sum, for whom she would watch anxiously as she came on duty each day. When Ah Sum left she transferred her affections to the Chinese nurse, Pui Yee.

CHAN MEI

The emotional problems that Valerie and Wendy faced over Fung Tai proved even greater with their other teenager, Chan Mei. They were greater because Chan Mei, apart from Kin Nin, was the most intellectually able of all their children. She, more than all the others, was conscious of and frustrated by her limitations.

Taking in Chan Mei was primarily an act of love and

loyalty to Miss Dibden. Two of Miss Dibden's family of 76 were handicapped and therefore unable either to be adopted or to emigrate to England with "Mama".

Po Wai (Bobby), 12 years old and handicapped as a result of polio, was transferred to St Christopher's Home for orphans in Tai Po, though Valerie and Wendy continued to take a "parental" interest in him and he was a frequent visitor to the Home of Loving Faithfulness. In his teens he was able to get a menial job at the famous Tai Ping carpet factory, which had the advantage of offering him a place in a staff hostel. Later he moved to another factory job and shared a resettlement flat at Yuen Long, always making regular visits to see Valerie and Wendy.

But 15-year-old Chan Mei needed more care and supervision – and the two women promised Miss Dibden that they would always supply that.

As the oldest and only mentally handicapped child at the Shatin Children's Home, Chan Mei had occupied a particularly cosseted place in the orphanage hierarchy. Miss Dibden assigned her a team of little girl helpers who fussed around her, teaching her to wash and dress herself. From being the least capable child there, receiving lots of attention, Chan Mei experienced the upheaval of suddenly becoming, at Fan Ling, the most able child with little special privilege.

Initially she responded well and was happy and co-operative. But as time went by, growing understanding led to growing frustration at her situation. She could reason, but more imperfectly than most. She could talk, but was distressed at her frequent incoherence. A hurt mind battling in a limiting body, emotions developing with no satisfying outlet. . .

Temper tantrums gave way to obsessive behaviour patterns that challenged the patience of both women. Chan Mei became obsessed with her own hands, staring at them for hours and scratching, picking and in other ways abusing them. She began to pinch and poke the helpless children around her – possibly from jealousy, perhaps in an attempt to gain attention. Valerie and Wendy had to be firm with her as she became increasingly untrustworthy, especially with the smaller children. And when visitors came, Chan Mei would, by extreme or extravagant behaviour, focus all eyes on herself, especially those of any men who happened to be around!

The teenager began to talk about going to hospital. Perhaps it wouldn't be a bad thing for her to see a Christian psychiatrist, thought Valerie and Wendy.

"You're not doctor. Not wearing white coat," declared Chan Mei.

"Oh, I do apologise! I've just come on duty and forgot to put one on." The psychiatrist was quick to play along with Chan Mei, reaching inside a locker for a white coat.

At her own insistence, Chan Mei was given a thorough physical examination and prescribed some pills – vitamins. This visit appeased her, but only for a few months. She became more disturbed, demanding with hysterical screams and cries to go to hospital. Eventually there was no alternative but to have her admitted to the psychiatric ward at Castle Peak Hospital. Valerie and Wendy visited her regularly for a month, after which time she pronounced herself well enough to come home.

The improvement was short-lived. In desperation, Valerie and Wendy prayed about an alternative home for her. A weekday place was offered at the Tapella Home at Tsuen Wan, a home for a small group of more able handicapped girls run by a Roman Catholic father.

Again this proved not to be a long-term solution to Chan Mei's problems. After a year she was moved to an adult training centre - where she is still. This runs on a more formal classroom footing, interspersed with many outings. Chan Mei is still not altogether settled and has many ups and downs. Once or twice a year she comes "home" to the Home of Loving Faithfulness, and Valerie and Wendy make a point of visiting her every birthday.

The admissions of Fung Tai and Chan Mei to the Home of Loving Faithfulness family in 1966 meant it was bursting at the seams. The number of children – 10 – had of neccessity to remain static for several years of hard work and caring.

But within a few months the waiting list was over 50. And growing.

Both women had always felt that the bungalow at Fan Ling was only a beginning.

"Before we ever started the work we believed that God wanted us to have 80 to 100 children to care for. So even before the bungalow was full we were always looking out for a bigger house," says Wendy.

The intitial three-year lease on the bungalow came to an end and was renewed. Then came the time when the landlord announced his intention to double the rent. Or he would consider selling it to them – at a grossly inflated price. Valerie and Wendy assured the landlord that they would vacate his premises by the expiration of the lease – 31st July, 1971.

THROUGH NEW EYES
Of course, that old house in Kwu Tung village just outside Sheung Shui, the one they'd looked over before, was still an option.

The suggestion was dismissed. Even then the house and garden had been run down, decaying and filthy. What unimaginable state would it be in now?

Valerie and Wendy remembered looking over the house five years before, following the old caretaker around as he struggled with the ancient padlocks, rattling bunches of rusty keys in an old tin. It was large, but with a confusing, impractical layout. It bore none of the hallmarks of having been a family home. Previously it had been requisitioned as British Army barracks.

Well, should they look at it again?

"As I drove through the gate God very definitely said to me – 'This is your new home.'" Wendy could hardly believe the message she felt God impressing on her heart and mind.

The house *was* five years more neglected, more run down, more filthy. The ground floor was being rented out as temporary factory units. In one room workers were assembling aluminium window frames; in another a group of women were industriously making candlewick bedspreads for export. At the top of the creaking stairs the succession of cramped workshops gave way to scenes of desolation. Doors hung off their hinges giving glimpses of echoing bare rooms with soiled and splintering floor boards and cracked, grime-stained windows. The garden was wild and overgrown, with, as Mrs Blackmur remembers, "elephant-high grass".

"The Lord doesn't always give beautifully-wrapped parcels," she adds.

Quite an understatement. But, simply, God gave them new eyes to see the house. In Wendy's words, "Suddenly it had a potential that it hadn't had before."

The rambling house and grounds occupied a corner site. Here the road out of Sheung Shui meets the Lo Wu road to the border crossing into China some two and a half miles away. Number 250 Kwu Tung Main Street, later to be re-named 7 Castle Peak Road. The owner having died, the property had passed into the hands of his sister and three grandchildren, one of whom was a Christian. The four had agreed it should be sold to some charity or Christian work. Hardly surprising, then, that they looked with favour on the interest of the two British women.

The house was on offer for $380,000 (a little over

£28,000 sterling or almost US$50,000 by current exchange rates). Valerie and Wendy, in the name of their newly-formed trust, put forward a deposit of $50,000. They would easily need the remaining $20,000 saved for immediate repairs. They undertook to pay off the mortgage in two years.

Life assumed a more frenzied pace than usual. The lease at Fan Ling was within weeks of terminating. A contractor was sent in to check over the roof of the Sheung Shui house and to make an upstairs room into a kitchen. That, together with some cleaning by volunteers and a little superficial painting, was all there was time to do before Moving Day. Two large rooms along a verandah from the new kitchen were designated as the children's rooms. They were linked by a slightly smaller third room with its own balcony which would in time serve as a good playroom for the more able children.

In the preceding months, a number of servicemen from the Royal Welsh Fusiliers at Gun Club Barracks had become occasional visitors at the Home to lend the two friends a hand. And it was at this point that they suggested sending the Home of Loving Faithfulness on holiday.

ELEVEN

Operation Cheung Chau – and Andrew's adoption

The idea of a holiday wasn't new. It had been put forward the previous summer, but the Hong Kong weather had been as bad as it frequently was in June – hot and steamy, with torrential rainfall and typhoons. So the suggestion was shelved. Now, why not remove the children for a holiday while the disruption of the move was going on?

The plan was to take all the children plus Wendy, their local *amahs* Ah Ying and Ah Sai, and a few volunteer servicemen, to stay in four flats the Army owned on the tiny island of Cheung Chau, less than a couple of hours by sea from Hong Kong. Valerie would help them settle in and then return to supervise the move from Fan Ling to Sheung Shui.

Again a typhoon threatened to upset the plan, but after a couple of days' postponement the skies cleared and the operation began.

"We had to take an enormous amount of equipment – cots, mattresses, bedding, clothing, towels, physiotherapy mats, medical supplies, food, our pressure cooker and spin-drier. The Army sent a three ton truck and a coach. We wondered if we would ever get away. Loading all the equipment took ages, and that morning Fu Fu had a fever and we felt anxious about him.

"We drove to Sham Shui Po on the waterfront and then onto a land-sea vessel which was going to take us straight onto the beach at Cheung Chau. The children were laid on the physio mats. Somehow a large wave came over and we were all swamped. It was an intensely hot day and no one had thought to bring drinks."

The vessel arriving on the beach was quite a spectacle, attracting crowds of local people. Somehow the operation lacked military precision. "Pandemonium" was how Wendy described it.

Well into the evening the unpacking was incomplete. In all the confusion Wing Kit pulled over Ngan Ying's chair and she was unconscious for a few minutes. Fearing convulsions, the women took her into the next room to pray.

"I felt like going back," recalls Wendy. "How could we face a fortnight like this? When we tried to get the children bathed and ready for bed we found there was no hot water – the gas cylinders weren't working. The spin-drier would only function from one socket, which meant standing it in the middle of the sitting room. The typhoon of the week before had taken out most of the windows in two of the flats. And there was no phone."

Meanwhile, Fu Fu's temperature had climbed to 105 degrees. Wendy carried him off to the casualty department of the local hospital. After the inevitable delay, a doctor prescribed daily injections for four days. The boy vomited all night. Torn between his needs and anxiety about Ngan Ying, Wendy didn't sleep at all. The pattern was set for the fortnight's "holiday" that was more a nightmare.

The servicemen were less than helpful, regarding their assignment as an opportunity to get in a little swimming, rowing and relaxing on the beach. The two Chinese girls, Ah Ying and the newer recruit Ah Sai, couldn't be persuaded to take much of a share in the work, either. After all, wasn't this supposed to be a holiday?

So Wendy found herself weighed down with the practical duties of caring for all ten children. If it had not been for Robert, she felt she could never have got through at all.

Robert was a rather shy, tall and loose-limbed soldier with a mass of fair hair that waved over his forehead. In his off-duty hours he had become one of the Home's most frequent visitors, drawn especially to little Shaan Shaan. He was a 20-year-old carpenter, working and saving hard with the dream of owning his own garage one day.

Robert was caring and reliable. And Wendy needed his help desperately as the gruelling "holiday" progressed.

That first weekend brought another typhoon, which swamped the pretty beach and put sunbathing out of the question.

Then the press arrived in force. After all, it was a good human interest story: 'British servicemen give super holiday to handicapped children' was a great headline. Tight-lipped, Wendy refused their requests to carry the children down onto the sand to pose.

That night it was, as usual, past midnight before she had finished all the chores. As Robert gave her a hand with washing the dishes, she wondered aloud about how the newspapers had heard about the "holiday".

"Oh, that's the Major. You know — the one who's organised all this. It's that award he's working so hard for. He has to make sure he gets the right media attention."

That was the final straw. Exhausted and fearing one of the terrible migraines from which she'd begun to suffer, Wendy shut herself in her room and wept. To think that she'd believed that the Major had organised all this out of genuine concern for her, for Valerie and for the kids. Was it really nothing more than a selfish publicity stunt? Did no one, then, love the children for the children's sake but only for their own motives? The faces of all the people who had helped over the past six years loomed in front of her. Was she to believe selfishness of all of them? She felt betrayed and unbearably sad.

Misery hung around her like a black cloud the next day, even though she tried to pull herself together for the sake of the children. Robert was depressed, too.

"He knew he'd hurt me. But I couldn't comfort him, I felt so low myself. The awful thing was that, after months of talking to Robert about Christianity, that week he'd been asking lots of questions. But when he tried to talk about it now I couldn't cope. I said we would talk when we got back home, that it was just too distracting here."

Weeks later, there was time to sit down with a Bible and talk and pray together. And it was when another young volunteer, Peter, came to work at the Home for a while and took Robert out to a Bible study meeting that Robert was truly converted. Later God called Robert out of the Army to work with handicapped children. He was baptised at the Stanley Park church, trained at St Mary's Hospital – during which time he met the Canadian girl he was to marry – and now works with the handicapped in Ontario, Canada.

While Wendy described the Cheung Chau holiday as "pandemonium", Valerie summed up the house move as "a pantomime".

"There were a number of disasters – like the cooker that was dropped and the refrigerator that couldn't be got up the stairs. The worst part, though, was transporting all our dozens of chickens, cats and dogs. We had to try to keep them safe and separate from each other, so they were shut up, clucking, yowling and growling, all in different rooms."

Dozens of chickens, cats and dogs? From the very early days at Fan Ling, Valerie and Wendy constantly discovered abandoned animals by the roadside or in rubbish bins. In their first year alone they recorded discovering over 1,000 little creatures – kittens, puppies, pigs, chickens, ducks. And some they couldn't resist keeping. Many were great companions to them and the children and of definite loving and therapeutic value to the whole family.

ANDREW'S STORY – PART 2
Children have a habit of growing up. Andrew, who had been little Kin Nin and who had twice almost but not quite been part of a family of his own, was the youngest of the Home of Loving Faithfulness children. The move

to Sheung Shui took place just after his eighth birthday. Alongside their awareness that he was mis-placed in the Home because of his terrific progress towards "normal" achievements was the love that both Valerie and Wendy felt for him.

"We had begun to think that one of *us* should apply to adopt him," says Wendy. "Then, in all the chaos of moving, the idea was shelved."

One day Andrew was helping Wendy around the house. As they were making beds together and chatting, Andrew called her 'Mum.' "Andrew, do you realise what you just called me?"

"Yes."

"Andrew, would you like me to be your Mum?"

"Yes."

Valerie battled inwardly over this. She loved Andrew, too, and it was hard to release him to Wendy. "But," she says, "in the end I believed that God had chosen the right person to be his mother."

The adoption was processed without a hitch, and finalised at a court hearing in April, 1972. Within a few days the boy was admitted to the special education unit at Beacon Hill School in Kowloon – registered as Andrew Blackmur.

TWELVE

Painful Disharmony – And More About Susie

The letter, from a district nurse Valerie and Wendy had met at Capernwray, was read with joy. Janet wrote that she believed it was right for her to come to work at the Home to give her two friends the possibility of a break. Ah Ying having left, Valerie and Wendy were on their own – and tired. Janet next wrote that she was anxious about her flatmate, a telephonist called Shirley. Since the flat was provided with Janet's job, her imminent departure meant that Shirley would be homeless. She asked Valerie and Wendy to pray about Shirley's future.

If the two friends had been able to read between the lines of Janet's letter, it would have been revealing. And it might well have prevented a great deal of heartache. What Janet didn't admit was that Shirley was something of a liability and their relationship was far from easy. Shirley was a possessive friend, and rather too dependent on her. In fact, Janet had initially looked to the move to Hong Kong to make a break. But her concern for Shirley, a Welsh girl with an unhappy home background, motivated her to make the suggestion to Valerie and Wendy that Shirley might come with her. Quite likely her heart sank when Wendy wrote to say that, if the Lord was calling her, then Shirley would be welcome.

It seemed a happy arrangement to Valerie and Wendy. After all, they had already learnt the hard way that threesomes don't always work. Two close friends coming together seemed a sensible proposition. They gave them a warm welcome. Janet, with short dark wavy hair, was quiet-natured. She quickly established herself as a good worker with the children, and she was equally happy to do cooking and cleaning. Bespectacled Shirley, with light brown hair and a warm personality, was also always ready to do anything to help and was very confident with the children.

But it was only a matter of weeks before the seeds of disharmony were being sown. Quite simply put, Valerie and Janet quickly formed a close friendship which inflamed Shirley's ready jealousy.

In retrospect it's easy to analyse everyone's mistakes. The relationship between Valerie and Janet began innocently enough when Janet needed someone to confide in about problems between her and Shirley. Valerie and Janet established a pattern of meeting together frequently to discuss things and pray.

"Probably," says an older and wiser Valerie, "this was quite the wrong thing to do. All four of us should have got together to talk and pray openly."

"At the beginning I wasn't worried about the close relationship between Valerie and Janet," remembers Wendy. "The two were alike in temperament and got on well. I didn't think of it as being exclusive until later. I didn't realise for some time how jealous Shirley was, and how she was often missing for meals or would be found crying somewhere."

Wendy's reaction was to try to remove herself from the situation with the intention of being objective. But she couldn't help feeling sorry for Shirley. She could see that the closeness of the other two was proving very hurtful to her.

"I thought that by staying outside of it all, Shirley would be able to confide in me. Unfortunately, what happened was that Shirley fed her jealousy into me – something I had truly never experienced before. I found I was feeling excluded, too. I began to think about the terrific relationship I'd had with Valerie before Janet and Shirley came."

A household of four women and feelings running deep. Long hours, a demanding workload and minimal privacy. It was easy for introspection to set in. Casual words were magnified. It was perhaps Shirley, struggling with feelings of inferiority, who became the real victim, although no one was to emerge unscarred. One day Shirley walked out. The note she left was discovered in time to track her down and it was Joann – now back in Hong Kong and re-established as a friend to the Home – who took her into her flat, counselling and comforting her until she felt able to return to Sheung Shui.

When Janet and Shirley knew the ropes, Valerie took her first home leave. That might have solved some problems but it didn't, as her close friendship with Janet continued by post. Shirley became obsessive about this, even to the point of taking Valerie's letters from Janet's room. She was still spilling out her jealous complaints to Wendy.

Wendy, recovering from eye surgery (the intense migraines she had been suffering from had turned out to be symptoms of glaucoma) began to dread Valerie's return because of the relationship problems. She was sad and disillusioned.

"I couldn't believe our wonderful relationship had come to this point of total lack of communication. We were like strangers. When I thought of all we had so far gone through together, I couldn't understand it."

There were other problems, too. Wendy, still new to the role of Andrew's mother, found that the boy's different position in the household wasn't really respected. Shirley, for instance, was a strong disciplinarian and seemed constantly to undermine Wendy's different way of mothering.

When Valerie did return from leave she quickly noticed that Shirley's hurt feelings were being expressed in bad temper towards those entirely without blame – the defenceless children and animals at the Home. Then one day Shirley slipped while closing windows during a storm and hurt her back. An initial need to rest became an excuse to avoid work, which only added to building resentments.

No one was prepared, though, for Shirley's attempted suicide.

How much this was a serious attempt to end her life and how much a cry for help is hard to determine. Shirley had easy access to the drugs at the Home as she regularly took pills to control her epilepsy. But late one night she took enough phenobarbitone to kill herself three times over.

As soon as she had taken the lethal overdose, Shirley went to find Janet, confessing what she had done and begging her not to tell anyone. Janet, terrified, ran for Wendy, and together they tried to make Shirley vomit.

Wendy bundled her into the car just as Valerie woke and ran out onto the balcony.

"What's happening?"

"Janet will tell you", called Wendy, swinging the car out through the gate.

Shirley began vomiting on the way to the clinic, and once there the staff made her drink six or seven pints of water before sending them on to hospital where Shirley was admitted for observation.

When Wendy returned to Sheung Shui, the three sat around silent and shocked. Wendy kept hearing in her mind Shirley's insistence that she no longer knew God. She was fearful of what impact the attempted suicide might have on the Home and the children they loved. Fortunately the hospital staff had agreed not to put her in the custodial ward, so possibly this would avoid police involvement. But what if this came out into the open – into the newspapers, perhaps?

Janet visited the next day, taking Shirley her Bible, which she refused. After a few days she was discharged and went to stay with some friends. With Shirley away the tensions lifted a little. But all three remaining were exhausted and drained. Valerie, in particular, could scarcely do any of her duties – and then it was discovered that she had, for a second time, a slipped disc. She spent several weeks in traction before returning home in a plaster cast.

THE LORD'S ENCOURAGEMENT

Amazingly, it was at this time of great pressure and even depression that both women testify to experiencing real encouragement from God. This included them both receiving the spiritual gift of tongues. They needed this vital strengthening of their faith to face the continuing relationship crisis.

With Valerie's health restored, there was no reason why Wendy should not take some much-needed leave. She went to see Shirley before she left, still hoping that there had been a change of heart and that she might be reconciled and resume working at the Home. But that was not to be. Shirley seemed hard and distant, and was convinced that she had lost her faith.

"She told me she couldn't pray. She didn't seem to be broken over her experiences; she was even self-assured."

Later Valerie spent time with Shirley and reported her quieter and more peaceful. "We had a lot to learn about love. And about criticism," says Valerie. "For my part, I had to learn that it was God's business to change people, not mine. And I had to learn acceptance of others. It was a purifying experience.

"There are a lot of stresses in community life. We were constantly together. It's not even like the husband-wife relationship because mostly the husband goes off to work each day."

"We needed to learn not to be so critical," agrees Wendy. "Satan wants us to be introspective."

Throughout this period of emotional turmoil, care for the children continued, of course, the women doing their utmost to maintain the highest standard of love and care for them. But the lives of the children, too, were not without their own crises during this time.

SUSIE – PART 2

The breakthrough in Susie's feeding achieved on that significant day spent on the rooftop of the YMCA and in a playground on Victoria Peak, though wonderful, was no permanent victory. After some time the battles over feeding of their brown-blotched but lovable Susie resumed with growing intensity.

A dramatic new phase of Susie's life began during the period of Valerie's first leave. Janet and Shirley were working, and Wendy was spending a day off with her adopted son, nine-year-old Andrew, and her mother. Mrs Blackmur was now living in Hong Kong. Having retired from the civil service she had been invited to move out to Hong Kong by her son Michael when he was re-located there by his company. With both her children in Hong Kong there was no reason for her to hesitate in Thornton Heath, London. So she was now living at Clearwater Bay in Kowloon, with Michael, his wife Elaine and grandson Robert, and paid frequent visits to the Home, where she was at first "Aunty Liz" and later simply "Grandma".

On the day in question Wendy was taking Andrew to a children's fancy dress party.

"As we were driving along Waterloo Road the heavens opened, without warning. The rain was so heavy we had to stop the car and pull over into a side street.

"It was an area where there were lots of roadworks in progress and the torrents of water added to the chaos. Police were turning people back and I was worried we'd be late for the party.

"I decided to double back past the Home and try another route. But, passing the Home, I had a strong feeling I should stop. I found Susie was not at all well, with a high fever. Andrew never did get to the party

— I had to leave him and dash off with Susie to the hospital."

It was the beginning of a nightmare.

Whenever a child from the Home of Loving Faithfulness had been admitted to hospital previously, Wendy and Valerie had discovered a wonderful ally in Dr Johnson Lee. He was a caring man who had always taken a special interest in their children. Even mentioning his name to hospital staff ensured they were given good treatment. Wendy had no qualms about such name-dropping — she felt their children needed special care.

But, on arrival at the hospital with a very sick Susie, Wendy found that Dr Lee had left to go into private practice.

The difference in care was soon apparent. Susie — so small and blind that they lovingly referred to her as their "little mole" — spent the next few weeks shuttled from ward to ward in different hospitals, the victim of continual changes of mind as to the true diagnosis of her weakening condition. She had pneumonia. No, it was typhoid. Well, perhaps it was pneumonia after all.

It was a dreadful, harrowing time, especially for Wendy. She herself was recovering from a second eye surgery and was supposed to be taking life easy. But she expended enormous amounts of time and energy rushing around from hospital to hospital trying to oversee what was happening to her beloved Susie. Twice Wendy was ordered to hospital immediately, on the grounds they thought the child was about to die. And the carelessness and neglect — unexplained bruising, undressed bed sores, her fluid intake unmonitored, her airway tube blocked and uncleaned for hours — to which poor Susie was subjected was a source of constant pain to Wendy.

"I couldn't believe this was all happening. A child's life was at stake! But, you see, Susie was retarded. They didn't think it mattered whether she lived or died. It was clear to me that they were just leaving her to die. It was the kind of attitude I met in medical circles again and again."

In desperation Wendy made an appointment to see the ward doctor. The evening before, she went to St Andrew's Church to see the vicar and his wife, Bob and Helen Hyatt. They discussed Susie's problems and spent some time praying. Wendy resolved to ask the ward doctor to allow the child to be transferred to the Ruttonjee Hospital on Hong Kong Island. It would be highly irregular. But Sister Gabriel there agreed to take her and Wendy was convinced that the Roman Catholic sisters who ran the Ruttonjee would be sensitive to the little girl's needs and hurts. She wanted the months of neglect ended.

Wendy was on the ward early the next morning in good time for her appointment with the doctor. She knew she needed a miracle. No, several miracles: not only the doctor's permission for the transfer, but the hospital authority's willingness to provide the ambulance complete with the oxygen and drip equipment that were vital if Susie was to survive the journey to the Ruttonjee.

Wendy foiled an attempt to head her off from seeing the doctor, refusing to accept the "he's so busy" from the nurse.

Once face to face with him there was little evidence that the doctor would comply with her request.

"I can't sign her off. She'll die if you transfer her."

"But, doctor, she'll die if she stays here!"

More words. No progress. Wendy turned to go. "Miss Blackmur, if you were to insist on taking her, she would cease to be our concern. The minute she was outside the ward door then she would be entirely your responsibility. I can't allow that. Is that clear?"

"You've made it very clear, doctor."

Her hand was on the door handle. What should she do?

"However. . ."

There was a pause.

"However, you can go to see the paediatric specialist. Get his opinion."

Wendy took a deep breath and headed down the corridor. Ignoring the receptionist she went straight into the specialist's room without knocking.

The man behind the desk was talking on the phone in Cantonese. Talking, Wendy recognised straight away, about Susie's condition. Concealing her understanding, she waited, expressionless. He motioned her to take a seat.

The phone call complete, Wendy tensed for battle. But she didn't really get one. Hearing her out, the specialist agreed that she could have Susie transferred.

Not even then was it a straightforward matter. The Hong Kong weather, which so often seemed to conspire with the enemy, was building itself up into a typhoon. The Number Three warning signal had just been hoisted – meaning that no ambulances could cross the harbour. They were ordered to return to base to await emergency calls.

There was only one hope. One ambulance from Hong Kong Island had brought over a patient to Castle Peak Hospital on Kowloonside. If it could be intercepted on its way back to the Island then Susie could be picked up en route.

Praying desperately, Wendy contacted the Ruttonjee and asked them to get a room ready for Susie. And arranged for contact to be made with Susie's mother to tell her about the transfer.

It all worked. The ambulance was intercepted and pulled up in the driving rain as Jo arrived with Susie's mother.

Arriving at the Ruttonjee, Susie was laid tenderly on the waiting bed. She gave a tremendous sigh. Within an hour she was off oxygen and breathing normally.

From that time the Home of Loving Faithfulness never allowed any of their children to be admitted to government hospitals, convinced that the staff would not be able to offer the kind of specialised care their children needed. At least, there was one other time, one other child. . . and a tragedy. . . but that account comes later.

And so does the end of Susie's story.

THIRTEEN

Plus Five Make Fifteen – and Wendy Makes a Decision

The children admitted to the Home of Loving Faithfulness generally came from desperately poor home conditions. That's the way that Valerie and Wendy wanted it. They took joy in lifting some of the financial burden oppressing these families and did their best to keep in supportive contact with them when such a relationship was happily received.

Sau Ming's family, though, were not in the usual hurting circumstances. By comparison with most local people, they lived comfortably. And they were Christians who loved their youngest daughter, although at 19 she was completely helpless, severely epileptic and brain-damaged.

Had she been "normal", Sau Ming would have been a tall, handsome woman. As a child she had been able to walk and had some speech. But around the age of 12 her condition had deteriorated and her epileptic fits intensified. Seven years on, the potentially beautiful features were scarred as a result of the many terrible falls experienced during fits. Over the years she had become more and more physically helpless. Now she was unable to do anything more than suck her thumb – and give a gorgeous slow smile from time to time.

Valerie and Wendy were asked if they would care for Sau Ming for three weeks. Both parents worked – father was an engineer with a textile firm and mother had a fulfilling career as headmistress of a respected Christian school. Sau Ming was looked after by an elderly aunt who wanted to visit China for medical treatment. Attempts to employ an *amah* to look after Sau Ming had failed. Even at double salary it proved impossible to find someone willing to take on the job. The traditional Chinese mind strongly associates the mentally handicapped with evil spirits, and such a job was viewed through an oppressive cloud of fear and superstition.

Valerie and Wendy agreed to take in Sau Ming temporarily. The aunt's trip proved to be several weeks longer than the estimated three – but, never mind. Though heavy to lift and bath, Sau Ming was in no way a troublesome child.

When the aunt returned it was with depressing news of a diagnosis of glaucoma and high blood pressure that could not be medically eased. Sau Ming's mother reluctantly resolved to leave her job to care full-time for her daughter, although the school made desperate attempts to make her change her mind. She came to Wendy in tears, anguishing over what to do.

"'Do good unto all men, especially those of the household of faith' was the Bible verse that came to me as I prayed about taking her in," recalls Wendy. Sau Ming is still a much loved member of the Home of Loving Faithfulness. Though her father has since died, she continues to be much loved by her mother, who is one of the Home's most frequent visitors.

LO SHAN

With the addition of Sau Ming, the Home of Loving Faithfulness began another phase of its growth. During August 1972 12-year-old Lo Shan arrived to join the family.

Lo Shan, the eldest daughter in a family of six children, was microcephalic. Father was a police constable and the family lived in police accommodation – but their noisy daughter made for strained relationships with neighbouring colleagues. Now mother was ill and frequently hospitalised. Understandably, father couldn't cope.

Little Lo Shan spent most of her days sitting in her cot,

rocking to and fro. With her head thrown far back, her long thin limbs waving, and her stomach very distended due to her persistent habit of swallowing air, she brought to mind the vision of a cross-tempered frog. In time the ill humour subsided, though not her inflated tummy.

TWO SISTERS – SIU LING AND SIU PING

Siu Ling and Siu Ping, both severely retarded though with no identifiable syndrome, were the eldest of five children of a desperately needy couple living in a resettlement flat beyond Kwun Tong. They became the next additions to Valerie and Wendy's family.

The girls' father had worked in a garage, but struggled with diabetes which eventually meant he had to give up his job. Mother worked as a street cleaner on the estate where they lived. Seven-year-old Ling and her four-year-old sister Ping spent every day locked in a small room watched by a deaf grandmother.

Both girls were very demanding. Ling, the more disturbed of the two, was hyperactive and cried a great deal. Her little sister was blind and very difficult to hold as she would wriggle and thrash her arms and legs around wildly.

The sisters required a lot of patience. Ling, jokingly nicknamed at the Home "Moaning Minnie" because of her crying noises, could be very difficult and the way she grabbed people was physically quite tiring. Her younger sister was calmer, settled more quickly and made better progress. She was often called "Ping Pong" as one of her favourite habits was curling up into a tight ball and then springing open.

MEI HEUNG

One name which had been on the waiting list for over six years was that of a spastic girl, Mei Heung. Valerie and Wendy thought of her frequently and felt that with more space she should be admitted.

The child, now 14 years old, lived with her widowed mother. Years before, when Valerie and Wendy had visited them, they had been impressed by how attached to each other mother and child were. Mei Heung had been terrified of being separated from her mother, clinging frantically to her, and this was one reason for putting off her admission.

But now mother urgently needed help following the death of the elderly grandmother who had watched Mei Heung when she went to her job as a refuse collector.

Wendy visited them in their small but immaculately clean room in Shek Kip Mei. The child, very pretty and, in spite of incontinence, as spotlessly fresh as the room, spent her days sitting in a canvas chair, her nights on a piece of hardboard and a mat on the floor.

Mei Heung settled in happily at Sheung Shui. She had an attractive, cheerful personality and was soon greatly loved. Sadly, she spent just eleven months at the Home.

"One day, sitting in her chair, Mei Heung gave a loud cry and was seized by tremors — not a fit, but something akin to it," recalls Wendy.

Valerie and Wendy watched her carefully. Two weeks later she was obviously unwell, but a doctor was unable to pinpoint a specific condition in spite of a whole battery of tests. It was suggested that her whole system was simply and irrevocably slowing down — something the two women found hard to accept and yet impotent to fight.

The girl then developed a fever and within a few days was semi-conscious. She slipped quietly out of this life on Easter Sunday. The Home seemed empty without her.

A FAMILY OF FIFTEEN

Back in May 1973 when Mei Heung had arrived, the family had grown to 15 children. From their early Fan Ling days there were still 10: two girls of 21 — the skateboarding Fung Tai and the problematic Chan Mei;

impenetrable 17-year-old Laan Chan; giggling, chattering Ngan Ying, now 16; Wing Kit, an ungainly 14-year-old; Fu Fu, a long thin 13-year-old with gangling limbs; two 12-year-olds – Siu Kuen of the winsome smile, and the feminine little Miss Shaan Shaan; 10-year-old lovable and brown-blotched Susie; and the newly-adopted Andrew, now aged nine. The more recent Sheung Shui additions were all girls – Sau Ming (20), Mei Heung (14), Lo Shan (13) and the little sisters Siu Ling (7) and Siu Ping (4).

But, though the children continued to be nursed and cared for, all was far from well as far as the staff of the Home were concerned.

WENDY'S DECISION

Learning to be a mother to Andrew, coping with eye surgery, the trauma of little Susie's life constantly hanging by a thread, the stress of the continuing relationship problems between herself, Valerie, Janet and Shirley – all this, added to the burden of day to day nursing of the children, made life a constant uphill struggle for Wendy. Aside from emotional considerations, the practical timetabling of each day was an insurmountable clamour of obligations and deadlines.

Plans for Andrew to attend Beacon Hill School's special unit in Kowloon had originally been made on the strength of the willingness of another family to drive him to and fro each weekday. But when the family left, his transport became another daily headache. Always so much to do. So few hours in the day.

It wasn't easy for Wendy to have that special relationship with Andrew that she longed for. There were too many "aunties", often resulting in conflicting discipline which confused the child. The day's pressures robbed Wendy of those precious moments she wanted to spend with him. He had regained frustratingly slowly the ground lost during his unhappy time at Evangel Home.

Of course, Wendy was not the only one experiencing real inner turmoil as a result of the strained staff relationships. Continuing stress resulted in little communication between any of the women. But Wendy was experiencing a growing feeling she describes as being "removed" from the others.

She took the initiative of calling Valerie, Janet and Shirley together, suggesting that God wanted the breaches in their relationships healed, that they must admit their shared guilt and ask Him for forgiveness. The conversation that followed was a time of confession. There was prayer together and a real determination to begin again. But Wendy had more to say.

"I believe it's right for me to leave the work."

She recalls feeling "a sense of the inevitable" about this momentous decision.

"You see, I wasn't even close to Valerie any more. But mostly I felt I was going for Andrew's sake. It seemed as if part of the reason the Lord had given him to me was to take me out of the work. The work was so demanding that I hadn't been able to give him the attention he needed. Adoption hadn't really changed things for him and that was wrong. He was taking a back seat in my life. All during the time of Susie's sickness Andrew had taken second place to her.

"But there was more. I hated the atmosphere in the house and wanted to get away from it. I hated the mistrust. I hated worrying about the effect of what I said on other people, and not being able to be natural in my own home. So, yes, it seemed inevitable that I should go."

Hearing the news, Valerie was shaken but silent. The protest in her heart never reached her lips.

"I just didn't know what to say. I kept thinking that God must do something big in my life to enable me to cope without Wendy. I was thankful that Janet was a nurse and hoped she would continue with me. But it was impossible to visualise the Home of Loving Faithfulness going on without Wendy. Compared to her, I felt I was basically a much weaker person. I wasn't as competent in the language; I felt my mind wasn't quick enough. Surely Wendy would come back. Wouldn't she?"

FOURTEEN

Dearest to your Heart

Wendy and Andrew left for England in June 1973.

"I only had the money for single tickets and left thinking I might never return – something which devastated me because I loved Hong Kong.

"There was no joy in my homecoming, and I felt coldly received by my home church because of lack of understanding of what I was now doing. I had been over seven years in the work and felt that it was all over. I was relieved to be away; I needed a breathing space. But I was convinced that I was still called to Hong Kong and I met with no understanding of that. I was desperately short of money and felt bitter about it. No doubt I directed my hurt towards people. But I was driven by my desire to give Andrew a stable home. This was without doubt one of the hardest times in my life."

A significant part of her heart remained in Hong Kong. And particularly with little Susie.

"I left just as she came out of Ruttonjee Hospital and had real misgivings about how the others would cope with her. Janet was in a very nervous state. Would she remember Susie's injection regime along with her other daily duties? When later I had a letter saying that Susie had been re-admitted to hospital I would have got on the plane to Hong Kong immediately if I'd had the money for the tickets."

But there was no money. Then a friend gave her an envelope, saying, "Use this for whatever is dearest to your heart."

The gift, fifty pounds, could so readily have eased the day-to-day struggle to provide the necessities of life for her and Andrew.

"But dearest to my heart was Hong Kong. I sent the money immediately to Valerie. I had booked return tickets with a travel agency in Hong Kong and this would be part payment. I could cope with leaving the Home. But not with leaving Hong Kong."

Meanwhile, Shirley had left Hong Kong and Valerie and Janet were joined by a new staff member, Jenny. She was no stranger to the work. She had initially heard about the Home of Loving Faithfulness while working as a nurse in Singapore. She had worked as a volunteer during a leave one Christmas-time, while the Home was still at Fan Ling. After completing her nursing training in England, she now wrote to say she would like to join the work. Valerie, remembering how quick and efficient she was and how well they had got on, was happy to accept her.

Janet, increasingly nervous and tearful, was very apprehensive about receiving a newcomer. But it did mean that when Jenny arrived Janet could take a month off for some much-needed rest. However, far from easing the staff situation, Jenny's arrival ushered in a new chapter of problems for Valerie.

"Although I remembered her as an efficient nurse, I now found that she was quite slapdash in her work, to the extent that the children began to suffer from her rough handling.

"On top of all this, I was still dealing with Janet's tears and depression. And then the support money began to dwindle. I was plagued with thoughts that God was withholding provision because we were sinning."

From afar, Wendy viewed the problems reported to her in letters with increasing concern.

When she and Andrew had saved enough and returned to Hong Kong at the end of the summer, the decision about where to go was not at first a problem. Wendy's brother was on leave and the family home at Clearwater Bay was available. Later, Wendy went to stay in a friend's flat at Sai Kung.

But it was only a temporary solution. Given the use of Janet's car most days, Wendy spent the hours while Andrew was at school looking for somewhere permanent to live. Funds were very limited. Some days, after driving into Kowloon Tong to take Andrew to school, there was barely enough petrol in the tank for the return journey, so Wendy would park and spend the hours before school ended searching for her future on foot.

"It was the first time I had been dependent on the Lord as an individual. I discovered that there was much more faith required for that than for a work which was so obviously his. I learned to praise God in all things. . . things like when I lost the nice flat I saw in Yau Yat Chuen because I didn't have the month's rent to pay in advance."

As well as a home, Wendy needed a job. She was asked to consider being the superintendent of a Christian day nursery. The committee agreed on a generous monthly salary, with Wendy's working hours flexible enough to fit in with Andrew's school timetable. Thinking and praying about it, Wendy felt no call from God, and didn't believe it was a permanent position. But she was available and she was wanted. She accepted.

The accommodation problem didn't go away. Then, mindful of what Valerie was experiencing at Sheung Shui, Wendy suggested that she might move back to the Home to live. She would be prepared to help out during evenings and weekends. She had also in mind to take some of the administrative load off Valerie.

Living in, Wendy was even more acutely aware of the difficulties with Jenny. Emotionally and spiritually, Wendy was herself almost at breaking point.

"God, God, please show me what's ahead!" was her oft-repeated prayer. No answer came. Christmas 1973, spent with the family at Clearwater Bay and not with the family at the Home of Loving Faithfulness, was a wretched time. The festivities paled beside her concern for Valerie and for the children, especially for a sick Ngan Ying who was in hospital.

One morning early in the New Year, Wendy walked into the kitchen at the Home just before leaving for work at the nursery.

"What I intended to say to Valerie was 'Bye, I'm off.' Instead, out of my mouth came the words 'Valerie, I'm giving up working at the nursery and I'm coming back into the work here full-time.'

"I was shocked and horrified! I couldn't believe my own voice!"

During the day it dawned on Wendy that her inner turmoil had totally evaporated. There was a quietness in her heart.

Valerie, over the moon with joy, saved her tears till she could reach the bathroom. She'd spent a lot of time in recent months crying in that bathroom, or in the pump house in the garden pleading with God in prayer.

Wendy would not be released from the nursery until mid-March. In the meantime it was decided that she could take one of the large empty ground floor rooms at the Home to convert into a flat for herself and Andrew. With some gifts and the salary that she'd earned but had used only sparingly, the conversion work was done. The final bill from the local contractor, Mr Yeung, was just five cents less than the amount she'd saved.

When Jenny announced she was leaving within a few months, it seemed that at long last harmony would settle again on the Home of Loving Faithfulness.

SUSIE'S STORY – THE CONCLUSION

For months 12-year-old Susie held her own, making no tangible progress but causing no real concern. But then she was sick and went into hospital for a course of antibiotics. When she was ready to return Wendy arranged with the nursing sisters at the Ruttonjee to collect her after the weekend.

On Friday and Saturday they rang to see how Susie was. She was fine. On Sunday morning Sister Gabriel rang to say that Susie had died.

It didn't register. It wasn't possible. But it was true. As the nurse had been attending to her that morning she simply stopped breathing. No trauma, no warning.

Identifying her little body at the hospital, Wendy couldn't cry or be distressed. Susie just wasn't there any more. She was at peace and without pain at last. Wendy drove from the hospital with Susie's mother to the coffin maker. It was a special order. A box rather wide and not at all long. The hospital had decided against breaking her legs to straighten the twisted body, and Wendy was glad. She saw the only suitable box at the back of the shop. Plain wood, painted white. The coffin maker was asking $900. Relieved that Susie's mother was waiting out in the car, Wendy began the haggling that reduced it to $600. It offended her that anyone should be profiteering from a little girl's death.

That summer Janet went on leave to England. She wrote to say she wouldn't be returning. Jenny had already announced her leaving date. Wendy and Valerie looked forward happily to running the Home together again.

FIFTEEN

Faith and Finance

By early 1975 Valerie and Wendy were aware that they were approaching the end of the second extension period granted for paying off the mortgage. Some $200,000 was outstanding.

Wendy recalls, "Money seemed shorter than ever. And as the final due date drew near, the bank manager wrote to suggest that we should consider selling the house. With the large profit we would make – prices having risen considerably – he said we would be able to buy a piece of land and build new.

"But when we prayed about this God very clearly said to me 'My Name is over this house and it is not to be removed.'

"Talking it over with two friends who were the only ones who knew the true financial situation, it seemed quite clear. We had bought it at a certain price. We couldn't justify selling it to another Christian work at a profit. The only way we could make a profit was to sell it commercially. . . and then the Lord's Name would be removed from the house. We were all completely of one mind over this."

"So," concludes Valerie, "we finally wrote to the bank manager to say that we believed this and no other was the house of the Lord's choice."

Months passed. Prayer continued. The women believed that God would indeed send the $200,000, and they watched keenly for the postman each day. They discussed ringing the bank manager but didn't get around to it. What would they say?

Finally, three July weeks remained before the final payment was due. Then came a call from the bank manager to say he was coming to see them on 1st August – the day after the expiry of the mortgage. Definitely past the eleventh hour. He was shown into the dining room, where tea and polite conversation were served.

Then, quite calmly, he told them that three weeks previously an anonymous trust had paid off the entire amount outstanding on the mortgage.

"We both felt like falling on him and hugging him," says Valerie, "although on reflection we did feel a little surprised that he had waited three weeks before telling us the news!"

Wendy says she went mad with joy. "I dashed all over the house, shouting 'It's paid, it's paid!', leaving Valerie to be polite."

The incident was one wonderful example of the material answers to prayer experienced by the Home throughout its history. Some of these were dramatic while many were relatively small things – but all served to remind Valerie and Wendy again and again that the God they loved cared about their everyday needs.

"We learned to be careful, to enjoy the times of abundance without taking them for granted, and to rejoice over every gift, however small."

Back in 1965 with a family of 10 children in the Fan Ling bungalow, the work needed only a modest $2,500 a month (less than £200 sterling or about US$320 today).

Certainly many judged the Home spartan and the lifestyle basic. But Valerie and Wendy look back on them as "happy and wonderful days". They never ate any meat themselves, except for chicken occasionally, but they bought minced beef for the children. They lived on donated canned goods, and eggs from the market. They were never unwell and certainly didn't think they were hard done by.

They remember their joy and disbelief when the post on Christmas Day 1965 contained a cheque for $5,000. "It was an amount of money we had never dreamed of.

Absolutely wonderful! We made a point of being quiet about our work. We wanted to trust God for all our needs and the way to do it was to stay hidden and pray. We never advertised our needs – God was always the very best public relations officer we could ever have!"

One day the women were down to their last dollar, with rice and cans in the house but no fresh food and nothing for their animals. But the shopper returned from the market with a bundle of fish, a bag of fresh vegetables, several pounds of potatoes – and 90 cents change! Stall holders that day had found reason to give produce away free – something which never happened before or subsequently.

On numerous occasions donations arrived which exactly matched the bills outstanding. Sometimes it was a small amount to cover the telephone charges or petrol for the car. But there were other dramatic provisions. The day Wendy had a call from a Chinese man wanting to give her $10,000 she thought it must be a hoax. But it was for real – and checking the accounts she found it was exactly what was required to make up their shortfall in the next mortgage instalment.

The women were aware of a God who loved them and the children, and who knew of their needs even before they asked. Sometimes, they didn't even ask, but recognised the generosity of their Lord in the arrival of a carton of their favourite brand and variety of tinned soup, or in the offer of a playpen or other item wholly appropriate to the need of their children.

On the subject of income, Valerie and Wendy have always refused to take government grants and are also careful to take no donations for their work known to result from such activities as gambling.

Every penny of the HK$90,000 to HK$100,000 the Home needs monthly in the early 1990s (that's £6,600 to £7,400 sterling or US$11,500 to $12,800) comes directly, they believe, in response to prayer.

"Every month we have to meet bills for running our car and van, electricity, gas, medications, food, servicing our laundry and other equipment, school fees for those children able to attend kindergartens or day centres, and salaries for all the staff apart from Valerie, our nurse Pui Yee and myself," says Wendy.

"Sometimes we have gifts in kind – food parcels from churches at Harvest Festival time, for example, or pieces of equipment. But generally cheques arrive for hugely varying amounts from many different sources. In our early years, most of our support came from people we knew outside Hong Kong. Now most of it comes from Hong Kong itself, which really pleases us.

"Sometimes when we receive a particular gift we have no idea how the people giving it came to hear about us. Quite a lot of the overseas money comes as a result of people coming here to visit or to work and then going home and telling their churches about us."

Almost all the income comes from individuals rather than organisations, although the largest gift to date (HK$1.8million) was the proceeds from a 24-hour go-cart rally organised by one of Hong Kong's Round Tables.

Over the years there has been support from many of the territory's English-speaking churches, notably St Andrew's, Christchurch, Emmanuel, Kowloon Baptist, North Point and Cornhill Alliance churches, various Army churches and also the congregation of the Mariners Club.

Their attitude of total reliance on God to meet all their financial needs is one they have shared from the earliest days.

"When we started our work, we felt staggered that we were responsible for others, not just ourselves. But we encouraged each other and it was never a worry," says Valerie.

"We were often stretched but always knew that God would be faithful. Sometimes it's good to go without –

it reminds us to trust the Lord and that all we have is a gift from him."

Valerie protests that this "living by faith" doesn't make them "better" Christians. "When people say we must have great faith I tell them that this faith itself is not ours but a gift from God. Not everyone is called to live this way; God uses those who earn salaries and are in tune with him to support our work and other Christian ministries."

Their stand over refusing to take donations resulting from raffles, lotteries or other games of chance has brought them no small amount of criticism, and sometimes just plain puzzlement.

Valerie explains, "It seems wrong to us to take money from people who gamble for pleasure and gain. As far as we are concerned, it isn't glorifying to God. God doesn't have to rely on those sorts of proceeds to meet our needs. We are running a Home in the Lord's name and we couldn't take money from gambling and be comfortable about it.

"We know that in Hong Kong grants are available from fund-raising bodies whose income is largely the result of gambling such as horse racing. People have urged us to apply for these grants to finance our work, particularly the building project."

They have no problem saying "no" to such money – but sometimes saying "no" sensitively presents a problem.

"Some Christian organisations are happy to receive such funds – that's their decision. But we believe it's wrong for us," says Wendy.

"Sometimes we unknowingly receive gifts we later discover are from fund-raising methods we are unhappy with, and that presents us with a problem. On occasions we have been invited to public events to receive cheques for our work and been asked to draw winning tickets for prizes and so on, which horrifies us. Sometimes we have turned down gifts as large as $1 million when we have understood how the money was raised."

Faith and Finance

Another point of misunderstanding with some supporters has been the fact that Valerie and Wendy "tithe" or give away one tenth of all the income they receive to other Christian works or needy individuals.

Some also criticise them for the way they spend money on their children. They are generous in their provision of special equipment needed for individuals and in their celebrations of special times. In an effort to dispel the old images of the institution, each child has his or her own wardrobe of clothing – there's no common pool. By buying with an eye for bargains in the local markets they ensure that every child has attractive, comfortable clothes. And every Christmas, birthday and special event is marked with a new outfit.

"We see it as a form of caring," says Valerie. "We don't like our children to have secondhand clothes. I don't even like them to have odd buttons sewn on. We wouldn't accept that standard for ourselves, would we? It's all part of Christ's love channelled through us and into the children. We aim to give them dignity and an identity – whatever that costs in terms of money or human caring."

Birthdays are, indeed, celebrated with great enthusiasm for every child, no matter how handicapped. There is the excitement of preparation, the new dress or track suit, perhaps a haircut or even a perm with new hair ribbons and slides. There's always a party tea, the singing of "Happy Birthday to You", cards read out, kisses and hugs, cakes and candles, presents to be unwrapped.

And at Christmas-time each child has his or her own giant stocking – lovingly made by Grandma and decorated with personalised motifs – to be filled with gifts. These are usually cassettes, musical toys to hang from cots, mobiles or soft cuddly toys. For the more able there might be picture books or building blocks, a simple jigsaw, or educational learning toys. The children's rooms are hung

113

with decorations and echo with music. And on Christmas Day a little license is taken with the rather strict diets that need to be adhered to.

SIXTEEN

To Valerie – a Daughter

Dibs, an abandoned spastic baby weighing only 17 pounds at four years and eight months, was the only addition to the family in 1974. Two – Mei Heung and Susie – died, leaving 14: eleven girls and three boys.

Mei Ling joined them in early 1975, a mentally and physically helpless eight-year-old. Her mother's feeding technique had been to smack her or pull her hair until she cried, then shovel food into the open mouth. Mei Ling was to cry no more during feeds in the nine years she lived with the family.

After taking in Mei Ling, perhaps feeling overawed by the medical responsibilities of their growing family, Valerie was adamant that they should not take in any more children until there was a trained nurse on the staff.

Yet three other new children did come into the Home of Loving Faithfulness that year – a baby girl who was to make a significant difference to Valerie's life, and two little boys.

If it hadn't been for Ngan Ying being so sick that summer, Valerie and Wendy might never have found little Charlotte.

Ngan Ying, 19 by then, was admitted to hospital for treatment for chronic bronchiectasis. The doctor on the ward mentioned to Wendy that he was caring for three other retarded children in a side ward, so she naturally went to see them.

Of the three, it was the nameless baby girl who remained in Wendy's heart and mind. The child had been abandoned at birth and had known no mother's love surrounding her – the world that embraced her was the starched white sheets of the vast hospital cot, feeding tubes and remote uniformed figures. If only she could be loved and cuddled. . .

The tiny, wizened scrap of humanity looking lost in the cot was called simply "Edwards" by the nurses after the rare chromosome disorder (Edwards or Trisomy 18 syndrome) from which she suffered.

The child – Wendy called her Charlotte – was 16 months old and yet weighed just eight and a half pounds, the weight of an average newborn. Most babies born with this syndrome live no more than a few months. The condition is characterised by a long list of physical and mental deformities – heart defects, loss of sucking reflex, "rocker bottom" feet, malformed hands, and receding chin. So tiny Charlotte, having survived into her second year, was alive against all odds; something of an enigma. Or a miracle.

Wendy took Valerie to the hospital to visit Charlotte.

"As we arrived we met a missionary we knew visiting someone else. Charlotte was crying as Valerie went ahead of us into the room, although she was so weak you could hardly hear the pathetic little sound she made."

Valerie went straight to the cot and picked up the baby girl, a response which Wendy felt was an answer to her prayers.

"I felt she would not have picked her up if the missionary had not been with us. There was something about having that other person there that made her bold enough to do it – there's a kind of ease and familiarity that you put on when other people are there."

Looking back, Valerie had no recollection of the visiting missionary being there at all. She just knew immediately that the Home should take this baby. She was crying out for love, and Valerie felt drawn to her by a love which she sensed came from God.

Leaving the hospital, Valerie turned to Wendy. "Can we take her? Shall we contact the authorities about having her?"

This was certainly an unusual situation. Instead of taking a child referred to them, for the first time they were seeking out a child.

Charlotte's parents were traced. They lived near Kwun Tong but father worked away on the Portuguese island colony of Macau. The youngest of the couple's other children was 17. None of the family had made any attempt to visit the baby.

Valerie and Wendy began to prepare for taking in a new addition. The bank balance was low at that time and they could not afford any clothes for her. But, using two personal gifts of money, they managed to buy a cot and yards of pink and white material from which they made everything – bedding, night gowns and so on. A couple who were friends of the Home also gave some clothes for her.

When they collected Charlotte from the hospital that September morning, even the tiny dress they had made seemed too big and the first size bootees fell off. She was so frail and vulnerable. Both women felt an overwhelming sense of having taken on an even bigger challenge than usual.

They began with a one-hourly tube feeding regime. After some weeks they tried bottle feeding her but this was continually rejected and eventually there was more success with a spoon and then with a cup. After eight weeks at the Home her weight had increased to almost 12 pounds and she was noticeably more alert and active.

They knew that as an Edwards baby, Charlotte's prognosis was very poor. But Valerie and Wendy decided that they would just love her and thank God for her as long as He let them have her.

The following March Charlotte developed bronchitis and then pneumonia and was hospitalised in a grave condition. When informed, the mother, grandmother and sister began to visit her, the hospital she was in being conveniently close to their home. As she began to recover the family decided that the little one was now very "cute". Suddenly Valerie and Wendy feared they would lose her. Was the family that had abandoned her now about to ask for her return? Of course, that option was legally open to them.

"Valerie," asked Wendy, "have you ever thought of adopting Charlotte?"

"I hadn't," says Valerie, "but from that moment on I began to ask the Lord to open all the doors if this was His will."

The next time Valerie visited the hospital the mother was there and Valerie lost no time in raising the matter of adoption. By December of that year the no-name, no-hope baby was little Miss Charlotte Conibear.

"Looking back, I thought there would be incredible problems about the adoption," says Valerie. "But as it turned out, there were none – it was our easiest adoption ever!

"For example, they asked to see my bank account details. At that time the balance was $14! They asked about income: I said I had none. They said what *could* I earn. We suggested that I *could* earn $1,000 a month. They were perfectly happy with this! I let the family know through the social worker that they could visit at any time, but they never did."

Charlotte, defying all medical reasoning, grew into a much-loved teenage daughter.

In 1990, while working on this book, Valerie said, "I feel God has given Charlotte to me as a trust, on loan, so she's very special to me."

Within a few months Valerie was called to surrender that trust. Suddenly, without warning, Charlotte's heart failed one Saturday afternoon in November. In the midst of the desolation of her heartbreaking loss, Valerie was able to recognise God's comfort through the devotional passage she'd read that very morning. They were these words by one of her favourite writers, the missionary Amy Carmichael: "There are many partings in life; never once are we promised the joy of long continuance together here, but 'our gathering together unto him' is a certain joy."

An anonymous poem given to Valerie some years ago is one that she still treasures.

> One little girl,
> alone in her world,
> surviving but not
> understanding.
> People see her
> as imperfect,
> like a broken toy
> that can't be mended.
> I can read the wonder
> in their voice
> as they ask
> why my hours are spent
> watching her grow,
> why my days are filled
> with loving her.
> Are you going to give up
> your whole life for her?
> I could answer,
> I know someone who did,
> and He's not sorry.

"Whenever we take in a new child," says Valerie, "we want so badly to make up for the lack of love they had in most cases before they came to us. We all felt – and me, particularly – that we should make up for the love that Charlotte lacked in those first 16 months of her life."

The Lord gave Charlotte 16 years of love in return.

"We've always felt that with our children love is as important as food. It gives them the will to live," says Wendy.

In this the Home of Loving Faithfulness family differ little from any children.

"Our children, like all children, blossom when they have the security of love," adds Valerie. "Without love our children would be just like the rows of blank, unresponsive faces we saw at Po Leung Kuk. God's love ministered through us to them makes all the difference. It makes them individuals with potential."

A number of their children have come from very unloving situations and have responded dramatically to the lavishly expressed love of their new family.

WAI MAN

When Wendy read through the case notes on her desk, she pictured a tragic situation. A young unmarried girl gets pregnant, decides not to have an abortion, but delivers a very retarded baby boy. The father of the child lives with them in a tiny hut. At the age of three months the baby develops a high fever, resulting in terrifying convulsions. Appalled, the young man walks out, returning only occasionally to abuse his "wife".

"When I read about the situation I longed to take little Wai Man, who was by then almost three years old, to give hope for a new life to the mother. I imagined an attractive young girl for whom things had gone terribly wrong and whose future was bleak."

In fact the reality proved rather different. The mother was dull-witted and slow, unconcerned about either her handicapped son or her situation. Grandparents had been doing their best to help, although Wai Man was often left alone all day and his epilepsy drugs forgotten.

But by that time Wendy's romantic rescue of the young mother didn't matter. They had seen little Wai Man, an irresistible little boy, placid and quiet. And they longed to have him in the family.

Valerie remembers visiting him in his grandparents' basement flat, a dingy area divided by dark brown partitions and totally without windows, where eight people lived with just two double bunk beds.

"Wai Man was always kept on one of the bottom bunks which was also used for storage, so he was more or less swamped by piles of family clothing. As soon as I spoke to him he smiled. He was so responsive."

Six weeks after joining the Home of Loving Faithfulness family, Wai Man had to be admitted to hospital with a dry cough and laboured breathing. There he vomited a tube feed into his lungs. For 12 days he was in an oxygen tent, his life hanging by a thread. But he recovered.

As for the young mother – she did get a new life. She married and had a little girl. She rarely came to see Wai Man. But his grandparents loved him and even after the grandfather died, grandmother came faithfully to see him until prevented by arthritis.

In 1990 Wai Man developed heart problems and breathing difficulties, requiring continuous attention. More than once the staff felt that his earthly end had come. But he came through it all, still giving his beautiful smiles; until the day in March 1991 when they knew that the broncho-pneumonia from which he suffered would be the means of taking him into the presence of God. Mother and grandmother were sent for and arrived a matter of minutes before he died peacefully.

CHE KIN
Che Kin, a six-year-old boy with Downs syndrome, was welcomed into the family at the end of 1975, bringing the number of children again to 15.

Che Kin's family were simple folk, very kind but rough and ready and not able to cope with Che Kin, who was diagnosed as being a low grade Downs syndrome. He was left all day strapped to a chair. Two other boys in the family were mildly retarded.

When he arrived at the Home it was soon clear that he had never been trained to do anything, not even to stand or walk or feed himself. He was naturally strong-willed and needed a firm hand. Battles over feeding were fought and won. He learned to say a few words. And at the age of nine he took his first steps, and from then on he loved to walk and would take off on his own at odd times. He had congenital cataracts for which he received surgery, but his habit of continually poking his eyes meant a constant series of infections. He was taught to play with toys attached to his cot, but as his sight – in spite of medical care – continued to deteriorate, he found it increasingly difficult.

YUN PING

By now Valerie and Wendy were gaining some expertise in dealing with very small handicapped children. Dibs at four years and eight months was just 17 pounds; Charlotte at 16 months weighed eight and a half pounds. Then in December 1976 they took in Yun Ping. He was eight years old but, amazingly, weighed just 18 pounds.

Horrifying home circumstances made the women flinch no more. The father, an illegal immigrant from China whose wife had just died, lived with three children at Cha Kwu Ling in something best described as a cave: pieces of timber flotsam leaning against a rock outcropping with a hollow space inside, reached at the end of a network of tiny alleys. When it rained a torrent of water slid down the rock face and into the little home.

Inside, the family's pathetic belongings – a clock and a few clothes – were tucked into dank nooks and crannies in the rock. And Yun Ping, severely mentally retarded and with spastic quadriplegia but blessed with a beatific smile, was kept on a narrow shelf right up against the rock wall. Like some tins of baked beans in a larder. He had fallen off the shelf more than once and had lost his front teeth. But when he smiled, it was as though a light turned on. Yun Ping was admitted as quickly as possible and everyone at the Home loved him immediately.

"He seemed to understand a lot. He would wait for you to look at him and then respond with his big smile. We used to call him 'Freddy the Fearless Flyer' because when he was on your lap he would stiffen and throw his arms out with excitement!"

Sadly, little Yun Ping's new-found love and care was for only two and a half years. He died without warning, in his sleep, in April 1979.

SEVENTEEN

A Committed and Caring Companion

Valerie and Wendy continued to run the Home with a series of local helpers, some of whom stayed only months, some several years. But when Pui Yee came, here at long last was someone committed and caring with whom they learned to truly share the responsibilities of their special family long-term.

Pui Yee, one of ten children from a local Hong Kong Chinese family, was sent to England as a young teenager to continue her education. A recent convert to Christianity, her ambition was to travel – and to become a nurse.

The family, who owned a factory business on Hong Kong Island, were not rich – indeed they had borrowed money to enable Pui Yee to chase after her dream. In London an introduction to some Chinese people running a restaurant in Kilburn gave her and two other Chinese young people accommodation while they went to language lessons.

Within a few months Pui Yee went for an interview at a hospital in Tunbridge Wells, Kent. The matron, hesitating over the level of the girl's fluency in English, advised her against taking the SRN course but instead recommended the shorter and less demanding SEN.

So Pui Yee became a nursing student. And when she was not poring over medical books she was practising the piano, or improving her English skills by reading her way through all seven grades of the Longman Simplified Texts. She passed her exams in all three areas – SEN, piano and English. Her next goal was to go on to become an SRN. She was completely taken aback to discover from the hospital matron that the higher qualification could not automatically be studied. She found she had to take another entrance exam. And she failed it.

In tears she went to her Senior Tutor, who gave her an introduction to a colleague at a hospital in Canterbury specialising in psychiatric nursing. There Pui Yee sat exactly the same entrance exam she had failed a fortnight previously – and passed! She could only attribute the course of events to the guidance of God.

During three years' training in psychiatric nursing Pui Yee matured tremendously, both as a caring nurse increasingly aware of social problems and as a Christian.

Following a year working on the admissions ward of a psychiatric hospital in Hong Kong to give her opportunity to spend time with her family, Pui Yee spent two years at a hospital in Croydon, Surrey. A holiday in Moscow and another trip back to Hong Kong preceded a return to Croydon to take a year's midwifery training.

It was during this time that Pui Yee heard a talk at a nurses' Christian fellowship meeting. The speaker was a young nurse, Joann, who had been working at a place called the Home of Loving Faithfulness. . .

"I remember Joann saying how beautiful Hong Kong was. I was surprised: Hong Kong was my home and I knew it well. I thought of it as dirty, stinking and overpopulated compared to peaceful and beautiful England!

"Then she began to talk about the Home and it really struck me as so sad that it was necessary for foreign missionaries to take care of Chinese handicapped people because there was no local provision for them."

Pui Yee's midwifery training had given her a new appreciation of the value of life.

"I was realising how precious life is, and how so easily a perfect baby could become brain damaged by being deprived of oxygen for a few seconds. A normal beautiful baby could become blind, deaf, mentally handicapped. I was grateful for all the normal functions that I was blessed with.

"During my psychiatric training I had visited a big ward of handicapped people and had felt admiration for those working there – but I felt I couldn't do it."

Pui Yee had no desire to work in Hong Kong, or even to stay in England. She wanted to combine her nursing skills with her ambition to travel. She had been wondering about joining the World Health Organisation, and had also made an application to work in Jordan, where she had a friend working in a psychiatric hospital. But twice her application to the embassy had gone astray.

"I decided not to apply a third time. I kept thinking about the Home of Loving Faithfulness, and then Joann came back to the nurses' fellowship a second time to show slides. The Home looked a really scruffy old place. I began to think that I'd love to go there and tidy it up, put some paint on the walls and get it looking nice, especially the awful laundry! I decided that perhaps I should take a year out of my career and do some voluntary work. So I wrote to Wendy and said I would like to give a year to the Home.

"Her reply was brief and told me little. I knew that it would be hard work and long hours. But I began to feel that God was calling me to go there. Over and over again the message I was hearing was that if you do something for God, then He knows your needs and will take care of you."

Pui Yee finished her midwifery exams and did several months' agency nursing to raise money for the airfare home. All too soon it was December and time to say farewell to her friends Sue and Sandra and the wonderful "open house" they had all three shared in Thornton Heath, Surrey.

"The day I left we went out in the drizzling English rain for a meal together at a Greek restaurant. Sue and Sandra gave me a gift of one hundred pounds! As I walked back

I felt willing and ready to go anywhere for God – I just knew that He was going to provide for me. As the sun shone through the rain I felt I was being warmed by God's peace.

"In Hong Kong I made a quick visit to the Home to see it for the first time. I felt fine about what I was planning to do. I even recognised some of the children from the slides. I was keen to get started, in spite of my family's reaction. My brother, whom I really respected, thought I was wasting my time and my training. He wanted me to go to university. My mother told me that after visiting the Home she couldn't sleep – she was haunted by the children's faces."

Wendy remembers well that first meeting in early 1977. "Pui Yee was so bubbly and enthusiastic, and I loved her as soon as I met her!"

And Valerie found her "so full of life, so positive, so unconcerned about the long working hours, and such an experienced nurse" that she, too, warmed to her at once.

Yes, Pui Yee was a very experienced nurse. How did she cope with working with the two "amateurs"?

"I discovered that it was me who was the untrained person. For all my years in hospitals, I now had to learn a whole new concept of caring. I was the one who felt helpless, who could not communicate with the children. At first I could not see that they were beautiful, as Aunty Val and Aunty Wendy described them. Now, in my eyes the children are all truly beautiful."

It was a time of learning for Pui Yee. Not just an adjustment to a new level of personal caring. But learning all the other aspects of the family life – the cooking, cleaning, decorating, sewing. The first year at the Home seemed to be all learning, so she felt she should stay another year to put these things into practice.

And Pui Yee was also learning to trust God.

"To begin with, I was living entirely on my own savings

as, like Aunty Val and Aunty Wendy, I wanted to take no income from the Home. That year I walked a lot to save bus fares! But I experienced God's provision.

"After the second year I asked God to show me what to do and I felt he showed me that I was valuable here, so I stayed on.

"After the third year I was thinking I should leave; perhaps I should get a paid job in a Hong Kong hospital and come to the Home during my time off. I heard about a job as matron of an old people's home and prayed about it. But the home found a matron and I felt God was telling me to stay. After that I decided to stay until God told me to go!"

During her time in the UK, Pui Yee had close links with the Chinese Church in London, which she maintained in Hong Kong. After her third year at the Home the church sent her a gift of money and asked her to send news of the Home. Since that time the Chinese Church has supported her financially and in prayer.

A HURT OF A DIFFERENT KIND:
HANNAH AND TIMMY
During the late 70s the Home of Loving Faithfulness served as a refuge for two special people with a hurt of quite a different kind from usual. The family extended its compassion to two young people who had been badly burned in terrible fires – Hannah and Timmy.

As a small child Hannah lived with her family on one of the remoter New Territories farms. When a piece of electrical equipment exploded outside her bedroom window, the three-year-old was badly burned and needed much difficult surgery. Now in her 20s, she was left with permanent physical disabilities caused by the contractions of the damaged tissues, particularly to her hands and feet. There was scarring on her face, and her eyesight had been seriously impaired.

A scene from 1960.
Valerie and Miss Dibden
with the children at the
Shatin home.

Miss Dibden
in retirement in
the UK

Above: Part of the old building in Sheung Shui which housed the Home of Loving Faithfulness family from 1971 until demolition in 1991.

Centre: Sin Yee celebrates her third birthday with an enormous mouthful of ice cream – a photo taken by the South China Morning Post at the Matilda Child Development Centre on Hong Kong Island.

Left: A born actress! Sin Yee with pink silk suit and bamboo hat.

Right: Adopted! Becky in the UK with her new grandmother, two brothers and two cousins.
Below left: And Becky in 1988 – quite the young lady!
Below right: Fu Fu, admitted on the very first day the Home opened in 1965, pictured in 1990 at the 25th anniversary celebrations at St Andrew's Church, Kowloon.

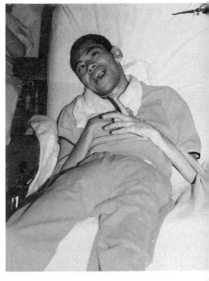

Right: Charlotte on her sixteenth birthday, giggling as her presents are opened.
Centre: Adopted! Samuel celebrates his fourth birthday with a party on the top deck of the Home's converted bus, shortly before leaving for the UK with his new Mum.
Below: Thomas and the cake made to mark his fourth birthday.

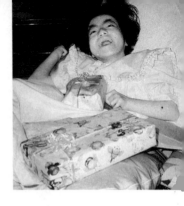

Above: Adopted! Nathan with his new family – Gregory and Helen and Little "J. J."
Right: Siu Ping with her favourite rag doll made by volunteer worker Edna.
Below: Nathan on his fifth birthday

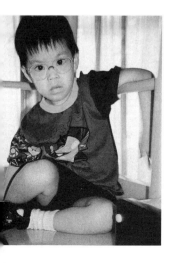

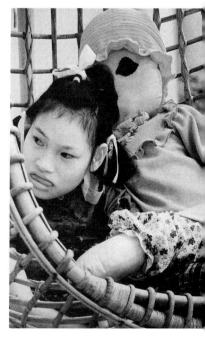

Right: Lo Shan in the early 80s with a YMCA volunteer worker.
Centre: Dibs enjoying a stroll with a volunteer worker.
Below: Yin Fan, aged 12, shortly after her arrival at the Home in May 1991.

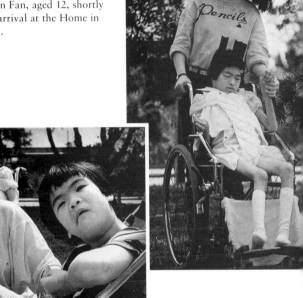

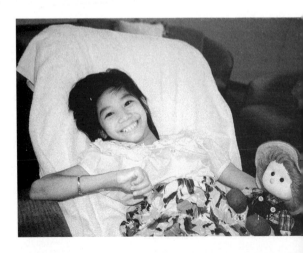

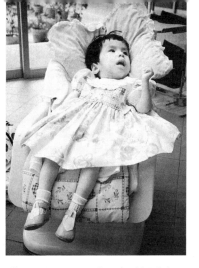

Above: Wai Mui on her third birthday, April 1991.
Right: Determined to manage her own breakfast – Yuk Lan, known as "Na Na", in early '91.
Below: Benjamin in July 1991, aged five months.

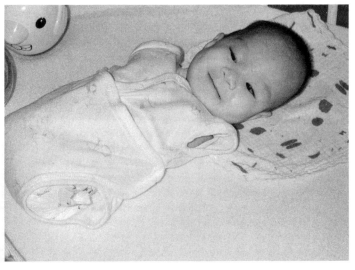

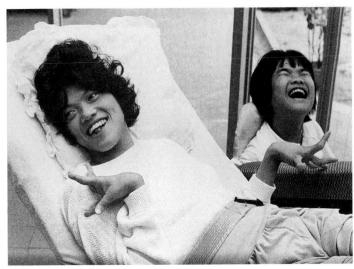

Shaan Shaan and Dibs – the best of friends.

Order in spite of apparent chaos! Mealtime in the children's playroom in the new units, with Marjan, a short-term worker from Holland

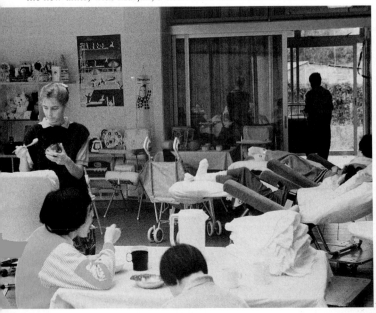

The family, who were Christians, had raised her in a cocoon of over-protectiveness. Now Hannah was asking to join the staff as a volunteer. Wendy and Valerie felt it would be good for her to get away from home for a while and be her own person.

So Hannah moved in and at first coped well with working with the children. In spite of her limp and scarred hands she was quite strong. But unfortunately Hannah's inner frustrations often expressed themselves in rough treatment of the children. After some time she left and went to work in the offices of a Christian radio organisation. Later she became an ordained minister in the Rhenish Church in Hong Kong, where she is finding real fulfilment.

The experience of knowing Hannah was good emotional preparation for the staff to understand and help someone else who was even more burn-damaged.

One day when the child Timmy was sleeping below deck on the family sampan, the boat's boiler exploded. His father, hearing his screams, rushed below to carry him out. In rescuing the boy he himself was fatally burned. He died a month later.

Timmy, massively burned, was also expected to die. But after much surgery and multiple skin grafts he survived.

"When we heard what had happened to this young boy we immediately wanted to offer our skin for grafting. Then we realised how silly that was, since he needed Chinese skin. But our hearts really went out to him and to his family."

When Timmy was finally discharged from hospital, his widowed mother was shattered. It was too painful to look at her son's grotesquely disfigured face, body and limbs. If she had to take him out she would lead him with a large brown paper bag over his head or cover up as much of him as possible with a sack to protect him from the shocked reactions of passers-by.

In his teens he was sent to the Cheshire Home on Hong Kong Island. Being with these chronically disabled people seemed the only place of relative acceptance for him. But missionaries visited him and offered him the love of Christ, to which he eventually responded by accepting Jesus Christ as his Saviour.

One American missionary in her 60s called Bea began to ask friends to pray that Timmy would be able to go to the States for corrective surgery. After seeing photographs of him, a surgeon promised to give his services free. A six-month visa was granted and Bea and Timmy left for the States.

All was not plain sailing. Timmy found the surgical procedures excruciatingly painful and emotionally traumatic. Sadly, one of the operations went wrong. The section of scalp transplanted to his upper lip supposedly to camouflage scarring with a moustache did produce hair – but it was wrongly positioned so that the moustache grew sideways. Timmy dug his heels in and refused to co-operate any more.

Bea wrote to friends in Hong Kong, including Valerie and Wendy, asking them to continue to pray for Timmy.

"This letter came while we had Hannah living with us. I realised that we didn't even see Hannah's scars any more – we had got so used to her. I talked it over with Valerie and Pui Yee. We knew that living at home was a problem for Timmy in that his relationship with his mother was so bad.

"We felt that Timmy could be very comfortable living with us. We were used to being with people who didn't look perfect. So I made a taped message to Bea, telling her about how we felt about Hannah, to encourage her. We told her we wanted to offer Timmy a home with us."

After some weeks Bea replied that Timmy had listened to the tape over and over again. It had given him hope. He was returning to Hong Kong and wanted to meet them all.

Wendy recalls, "As he stepped off the plane we saw him straight away. He was wearing a suit and a big flashy tie. I felt frightened. 'O Lord,' I prayed, 'What have we done, offering him a home?'

"But immediately she saw him, Pui Yee ran straight up to him and hugged him!

"One or two of his brothers and sisters were there to meet him, too. We had our big van so we all got in and we drove to the family home, in a resettlement room in Tsuen Wan. His mother was just sitting there with her head turned away, still unable to look at him. What made it worse was that Timmy's brothers were all so very handsome."

They left Timmy there, with an open invitation to come to Sheung Shui. The following day he arrived to stay.

The next hurdle was to find Timmy a job. Many companies wouldn't take him, on the grounds that other staff members wouldn't work with such a disfigured person. But then the Christian Literature Crusade bookshop agreed to take him on, at first temporarily but then permanently. He learned to make up book orders for delivery and also to man bookstalls for special events at church meetings, crusades or seminars.

Acceptance at the Home allowed Timmy to be himself. When he arrived, he was bitter and inward-looking. But he changed a great deal over the years.

"He's just a big miracle," sums up Valerie. "He has done marvellously well to accept the way that he looks and to let his own lovely nature come through."

Now he comes and goes, dividing his time between the Home, where he has a small room permanently allocated to him, and his family home, where, thankfully, his mother has learned to accept him as he has had to learn to accept himself.

Whenever he's at the Home he works – tidying cupboards, mending things, even helping Pui Yee organise outings for handicapped from the Home or from institutions elsewhere in Hong Kong. In spite of his claw-like hands he has learned to be amazingly dexterous, whether it's handling a screw driver, or picking up a handicapped baby.

THE CHAPEL
In 1977 the Home of Loving Faithfulness chapel was furnished and dedicated.

When they had moved into the Sheung Shui house Valerie and Wendy had designated a room for a chapel. But, with so much to do, it had lain untouched for years, though not forgotten. Then, during the Christmas of 1976, both Valerie and Wendy believed it was time to create a special place in the house for prayer and quietness.

It would be quite a big project. Mr Yeung, a local contractor, was asked to prepare an estimate for the work – a false ceiling, new windows, and replastering of the walls. Generally January and February were lean months for donations to the Home – but such was the women's conviction over the chapel that they gave the go-ahead for the work as a step taken in faith in a providing God.

"When the work got started I often went and sat in the shell of the room early in the morning as I prayed and read my Bible. We were amazed that there was a sudden increase in the amount of money coming in – and many of the gifts were specifically earmarked for the chapel," recalls Wendy.

"We were given a communion set with 40 glasses – exactly the number we had in mind when we first talked of registering ourselves as the Home of Loving Faithfulness Fellowship. And then we were given a set of old chairs for the chapel which we dismantled, painted and completely re-upholstered – again there were 40 of them."

They felt that in the creation of the chapel they were guided and provided for at every step of the way – from the choice of colour scheme, which was in shades of autumnal browns and beiges, to the provision of the lighting and curtains; from the crafting of a table to their own design to the buying of an organ at a bargain sale price. Then there was the decision to have Scripture verses etched on the two chapel windows: though Wendy and Valerie chose independently, their verses were exactly compatible in line length. "Having those windows was the biggest thrill to me. As I pray I can always look up and see the Word of God there – immovable and dependable," says Wendy.

EIGHTEEN

God-Given Families

As little Lai Kam was being born, her mother haemorrhaged badly and died as she squatted over the toilet in the family's Wan Chai apartment. Her tiny daughter emerged into the world with spina bifida, hydrocephalus and neurogenic bladder and was taken away to hospital. The father placed her two sisters in the care of an older couple who were unrelated but whom they knew as "Grandma" and "Grandad", and later took his own life.

Lai Kam was referred to the Home of Loving Faithfulness at a month old. Studying the case notes, Wendy felt the baby's continuing existence was something of a surprise.

"Spina bifida and Downs syndrome are the two conditions that many doctors worldwide count as not worthy of survival. Quite often a doctor will arbitrarily make a decision not to operate on a spina bifida baby but allow him to die. But Lai Kam, in spite of the difficult family situation, had been given the surgery that enabled her to go on living, even though a fair degree of mental retardation would result."

Sadly, there was no room for little Lai Kam at Sheung Shui when she was first referred. But there came a time when there was space for just a small cot – and then Lai Kam was the youngest on the waiting list.

So Valerie and Wendy set out to find out what had happened to her in the intervening four years, tracking her down by phone to a hospital. They were told that she was walking and talking. But she was in a TB hospital because she was incontinent. None of the children's homes would accept an incontinent child.

Wendy explained that the Home was intended for

severely disabled children, and if Lai Kam was walking and talking, she did not fit there.

She replaced the receiver and stood with her hand on the phone – "arguing with God", as she describes it. I felt God was saying, 'Are you sure she's not for you?'

For days Lai Kim remained on Wendy's heart. She rang back Lai Kim's social worker with a list of suggestions about alternatives to that hospital ward. Apparently they had all been tried.

Wendy and Valerie tried to imagine this child's life, confined to one hospital ward after another, year after year, with no enduring relationships, no real love. They felt traumatised just thinking about her. Yet she was far from being the kind of child they were catering for. They prayed and prayed. The Bible verse that kept coming to them was 'whom having not seen, ye love'. They began to love her without having even seen her. Eventually they felt that they should take her – because they knew they could alter her whole life expectation. At the very least they could give her love and a stable family.

Then another thought came. Could they be the means of Lai Kam being adopted into a family? Since the early disappointments of trying to find a family for Andrew they had never considered the possibility of an outside adoption again. But the message seemed clear. They felt that if God was saying Lai Kam was to have a family, then they could trust Him to bring it about.

After praying about it on a three-day retreat over Chinese New Year 1978, they felt confident about taking her in. God had promised her a family. They asked others to pray, too.

Wendy and Valerie went to collect her. Almost as an afterthought Wendy asked the ward sister, "Do you have any other children like Lai Kam?"

They were taken to see an abandoned one-and-a-half year old, also apparently with spina bifida. Later Wendy and Valerie agreed together that if God could find a family for Lai Kam, then they would take in this other little one, Tsui Chi, too, with the same intention of having her adopted.

Driving to Sheung Shui, four-year-old Lai Kam sat placidly in the front of the van on Valerie's lap, clutching the gifts they had taken and eating chocolate buttons. Apart from a little "oh" as they went out of the hospital gates there was little indication of anxiety over her changed surroundings. She settled in quickly and without fuss, though at first she was suspicious of the white faces around her and much preferred the Chinese staff. Her rocking, plodding gait was soon a familiar sight around the Home and within weeks she was happily attending a local Chinese kindergarten.

Staff and supporters continued to pray for a family. One English couple, both teachers, sometimes took Lai Kam home for the weekend. John and Jill had two boys of their own. It was the younger son who challenged his parents one day.

"You keep praying and asking Jesus to find a family for Lai Kam, Mummy. But why don't we have her in our family?"

Eventually, Jill, under tremendous conviction from God, called the Home to say that they all loved Lai Kam and wanted to adopt her. God had answered prayer.

Later Lai Kam, re-named Becky, was sent to Coney Hill, a specialist school for spina bifida children in England conveniently close to a loving grandmother, who could have her to stay at weekends. One amazing "coincidence": the Christian nursing sister at the school was on the Home's mailing list and recognised Becky immediately. She had been praying for her! In time Becky was to become a star pupil at the school, developing great artistic ability which won her several awards.

The rescue of little Lai Kam from a life bounded by a

hospital ward and the subsequent adoption of her as Becky was in every way a wonderful success for which much praise was given – and continues to be given – to God.

TSUI CHI
Could God do it again?

Tsui Chi arrived at the Home of Loving Faithfulness in May 1979, just over three years old. A life of confinement to a hospital ward was even less appropriate for her than for Lai Kam.

Tsui Chi was not really a spina bifida child. She was delivered at birth as one of Siamese twins. The other, a totally unviable baby, was attached to her back; and the operation to remove it left Tsui Chi with a damaged spinal cord. She could walk only with the aid of calipers and was incontinent. No children's home was prepared to take her. But mentally she was perfectly normal.

Tsui Chi blossomed at the Home. Wendy longed for her to be given some extra stimulus – preferably using the English language as, being realistic, it was far more likely that a non-Chinese family would be willing to adopt her. The ideal situation would be the spacious playgroup on the local army base. Wendy invited the supervisor to come and see Tsui Chi one lunchtime.

Wendy recalls the woman's arrival that day and read the tense expression on her face; she was obviously bracing herself to give a disappointing message.

"Miss Blackmur, I've been talking it over with the other. . ."

"This way, please. Tsui Chi is in our playroom and so keen to meet you!"

With a winning smile, Wendy ushered the playgroup supervisor ahead of her, not giving her a chance to say anything!

Wendy took her all over the Home, showed her everything, introduced her to everyone and left her, rather breathless, with the comment that she would bring Tsui Chi along to the playgroup the following morning. The supervisor found herself back outside the gate having totally failed to say what she had come to say. Wendy was sure that when Tsui Chi went along, not only would she be able to cope but they would all love her.

So they did. And it wasn't long before Sue, one of the Army wives running her class, became deeply involved with her progress and began to take her home to play with her own two children – who loved her from the start. When Tsui Chi got whooping cough and had to be isolated, Sue and the family came in to spend afternoons reading to her.

Soon Tsui Chi was more at home with Sue and Dick and their two children than with Wendy and Valerie. They were not surprised when the family came to talk about adopting her. Everything went through smoothly and they asked Wendy to choose an English name for her. She chose Rachel.

Sue and Dick were not committed Christians, but were so positive and loving to Rachel that Valerie and Wendy had no real hesitations in supporting the adoption. But when the family were posted back to England, communications faltered. And after some time a disturbing rumour was heard – that Sue and Dick had been divorced.

Wendy felt shattered. "My first thought was that the rumour must be wrong. Dear Rachel! Abandoned by her first parents; spending her infancy moved from hospital to hospital; finally so happy in a real family. Now? I agonised."

Letters received no response – nothing either to refute or confirm the reports of a divorce. So when Wendy next went on leave to England she felt she had to find out. She took up the trail on the army base at Chatham in Kent.

She was eventually put in touch with an army social

worker, and explained that her concern was for Rachel; she was not there to pass judgment on Sue and Dick.

Wendy left with the sobering truth and an address. There had been a divorce, and Sue had subsequently re-married.

She was able to contact Sue by phone, and eventually visited the family. She felt reassured and relieved to discover that Rachel was well and happy. Her new father, Tony, was very accepting of her. The resumed contact continued after that, with Wendy again visiting the family some five years later. Sadly, in 1989 Tony was taken seriously ill and died a year later of a brain tumour.

As for Rachel, she's now a bright young teenager coping well with normal school, although these days she needs a wheelchair for mobility because of increased spinal problems. All who meet her are impressed by how positive she is and how outgoing, involved in many activities such as Girl Guides and the church choir. Her ambition is to go to art school.

ROSS
Sonia was one of the sad casualties of the glittering but ugly city night life of Hong Kong. And so was the mentally retarded son that she bore.

In fact Sonia, a British woman, had given birth to five children. The first, an illegitimate son, was cared for by his grandmother in England. Then two daughters were born, one in England and one in Hong Kong, to Sonia and to her first husband. The husband was a nightclub manager, which brought them to the East. One day he went on a business trip to the Philippines and never came back.

Working as a bar hostess in one of Hong Kong's bright and bawdy clubs, Sonia struggled to make ends meet. Her husband refused to send her any money – but when she appealed to him for funds to send the two girls, Amanda and Tina, to England, he sent enough to cover their air fares. Amanda and Tina disappeared, but not – it was discovered much later – back to the safety of grandmother in England. Sonia, desperately in debt by this time, used the money meant for their tickets to appease some of the loan sharks who were hounding her, and secretly arranged for the girls to be put in a Chinese orphanage.

A series of casual relationships followed, more than one of which resulted in a pregnancy. A baby girl, named Samantha, arrived, and was largely cared for by Mrs M, a British friend with whom Sonia lived for a time. Then another baby, fathered by a western pilot working with Cathay Pacific Airlines, was born with Downs syndrome. Sonia refused to accept that the retarded baby was hers.

News of the little boy, named Ross, reached Wendy one day through a phone call from Mrs M. Mrs M, also a bar hostess and thankfully possessed of a genuinely caring heart, had been trying to help Sonia and was concerned about the baby. Ross had been ill, the medical fees were unpaid, and it seemed that no one cared. On visiting him, Valerie and Wendy saw Ross as a child full of potential and believed that, like Becky and Rachel, a family could be found to adopt him. Sonia agreed to sign her son into the care of the Home.

Admitted at the age of 15 months, Ross was very underweight but he was never a sickly child. Valerie and Wendy tried to encourage him to stand and walk, but he was nervous. For his second birthday they bought a little sit-on plastic horse on wheels, which literally liberated him within days. Soon he was scooting around the Home at speed, with an 'L' plate on the front of the horse, ducking under the high cots. With much time devoted to him by the staff, and attendance at a local toddler playgroup, he made attempts at talking, saying "An Ma" for "Grandma".

By this time all the paperwork necessary to make Ross legally free for adoption was being processed – and it wasn't all easy. Sonia had never registered his birth so there was no birth certificate. Hospital records had to be consulted to get the necessary documentation. Then, Sonia went missing. Even Mrs M, who was at this time processing to adopt Sonia's daughter Samantha, couldn't trace her.

There followed days spent tracking Sonia in the back streets of Hong Kong. Once found, there were delays with a mislaid ID card and passport. She would fail to turn up at meetings, but eventually the documents were produced and papers processed.

While Wendy and Sonia waited in an office during the final processing, Sonia confided details of her early life which helped Wendy understand her situation more clearly.

Then, to Wendy's concern, she asked to see Ross. Wendy knew this would be a hard moment for her. Ross had developed into a delightful toddler with a winning smile and gorgeous golden blond hair.

Sonia put her hand on his head. "His hair is so beautiful! Do you really think he'll be adopted?" That was all she said.

One morning Wendy was speaking at a Christian women's group. Prayer requests at the end of the meeting included Wendy's longing for a family for Ross. Afterwards she was approached by a woman with tears in her eyes, who introduced herself as Chris. She was a nurse and lived with her Army husband Gerry at Beacon Hill in Kowloon.

"Do you have a picture of that little boy – Ross?"

She looked at the little photo long and hard.

"He's my son," she said, simply. "Can I come and see him?"

Totally taken aback, Wendy agreed, though not without some hesitation. She arrived back at the Home only a short time before Chris and her husband drove up.

The couple took him into the garden for a walk, and then asked, "What do we do to adopt him?"

They talked at length. Chris and Gerry had two lovely

children, after which Gerry had decided to have a vasectomy, which they later regretted very much. They had tried, but failed, to get the operation reversed. For years they had been praying about a third child. They had contacted adoption agencies but had been turned down because they already had two children.

"When you were speaking today, Wendy, I just knew this was our child. And I did something I've never, ever done before. I opened my Bible at random and put my finger down on a verse. It was in the Gospels, where God speaks to Jesus and says 'This is my beloved son. . .'" Wendy was convinced. God was answering their prayer for a family for little Ross.

Chris and Gerry were to be in Hong Kong for a limited time and it was vital to get the wheels of the adoption bureaucracy rolling immediately. Their leaving date looked likely to arrive before the adoption was finalised. Because Ross was British the processing could continue from outside Hong Kong. However, they discovered they would have to start the whole process over again. There was no progress for months. Chris phoned from England to say they felt as if they were banging their heads against a brick wall. And then, suddenly, everything started to come together. Chris rang again, so much more optimistic. They were trying to arrange an Army "indulgence" flight for her to come to Hong Kong to finalise everything.

There were over 130 people on the list ahead of Chris for a flight to Hong Kong. But the Army staff member who arrived, newly-appointed that very Friday afternoon, to make the allocations of flights, not only knew Gerry but he knew the Home of Loving Faithfulness! When the situation was explained, Chris found herself top of the list. She flew to Hong Kong and in the two weeks allowed managed to get the court authority to take Ross to the UK for adoption.

With his adoption Ross became Samuel. In England he

was able to attend a special school. Over the years he has been a happy and much-loved child. When Gerry left the Army there were several fruitless years while he searched for meaningful employment but he finally found a teaching post in Oman, and Chris and Samuel joined him there in early 1991.

Valerie and Wendy believe no child, no matter how severely handicapped, should be classified "unadoptable", and are encouraged by changes in attitudes to adoption in Hong Kong in recent years among not only local people but also the authorities. At long last those with influence are allowing the adoption of children previously barred from families because of handicap.

But the two women don't underestimate the cost of adopting such a child.

"From my experience as a single adoptive mother with my own mentally handicapped child Andrew, I recall many times when I really felt like tearing my hair out," says Wendy. "I seemed to be carrying such a burden and I didn't know if I was going to make it. On a number of occasions I cried out, 'God, why did you give me this child?' As soon as the words were out of my mouth the question was also the answer. God *had* given me Andrew and so he knew all about it. He knew the kind of person I was and the kind of person Andrew was.

"One of the hardest things was when there were PTA functions at school. I felt terribly alone. One friend, Joan, sensed this and twice came with me. It was a tremendous encouragement and one of the most sensitive things anyone has ever done for me."

Aside from adoption procedures, there is room for more progress in the rights of the handicapped, for example in the area of their legal status.

All in Hong Kong carry an identity card. Those too handicapped to comply with the physical execution of getting such a card – getting to the office in person, negotiating the narrow booths to be photographed and so on – are issued with an exemption certificate. But this certificate only allows the issuing of a BDTC (British Dependent Territory Citizen) passport – which has no real validity after 1997 – rather than the BNO (British National Overseas) passport.

NINETEEN

Building for the Future

It had been "full house" at the old Fan Ling bungalow with just 10 children. At Sheung Shui the family had grown rapidly. The two large children's rooms connected by a playroom could take no more than 16 beds – 17 by squeezing in a small cot.

But then there was always the waiting list. And, bigger even than that, was the women's vision to help and love more and more children.

"We had always thought about building bigger accommodation. From the beginning God had given us both the idea of caring for 80 children," says Valerie. "So as soon as the mortgage on the house was settled we began to think seriously about building."

Why not just move to a larger house? A number of big houses were looked at, though none really seemed big enough. Besides, there was the conviction that this site in Sheung Shui was the place of God's choosing. And their needs were very specialised - existing buildings would not easily be adapted to suit the Home's requirements. What was really needed was something completely purpose-built.

The Sheung Shui house stood in a large unruly garden. Valerie and Wendy were amazed to discover that they actually owned 47,600 square feet in all. Other pieces of land on the market were looked at for comparison. Most leases contained the restriction that only a quarter of the total plot area could be built on. But, looking through the details of their agreement, they were thrilled to realise that they could actually build on two-thirds of their own land.

They themselves drew up a number of rough plans.

Always they visualised a number of smaller units rather than one large institution-type building. An architect teaching at the Chinese University gave the challenge to his graduate students. The scale and requirements were daunting. There would need to be live-in accommodation for 80 handicapped children and adults, and up to 50 staff. The whole project must be attractive, pleasing to the eye.

Valerie and Wendy were insistent that the new building would incorporate many features and facilities that were a direct result of their experience: special high baths that didn't involve staff in back-breaking bends when lowering children, for example; wide doorways to accommodate wheelchairs; plenty of light.

Finally, they approved the design ideas of a young architecture graduate named Joanna. It had the look of a "village", interestingly asymmetrical. The ambitious plan was for nine linked units surrounding a central courtyard. Of these, five units would house the children – 16 in each at ground floor level – with staff rooms upstairs. There would be one unit for administration; a laundry block with generator and workshop; a large kitchen with staff dining room; and a physiotherapy and medical block with a hydrotherapy pool.

They were obliged to put the scheme out to tender. Nine estimates were received. Valerie and Wendy were relieved to discover that the lowest was from the man they really wanted to do the work. Mr Yeung, a local self-employed man, had done very satisfactory small jobs for them in the past. True, he had never tackled such a large project as main contractor. But he was a conscientious and thoughtful worker who had proved himself trustworthy, honest, and totally sympathetic to the work even though he was not a Christian. There was no small amount of opposition to their choice from supporters of the work who insisted they were taking too great a risk. But Valerie and Wendy were adamant that Mr Yeung was the right man for the job.

Some money had been already set aside in a building fund. Confident that since God had never yet let them down, the rest would arrive when needed, Valerie and Wendy gave instructions for work to begin on the first five of the nine units.

But something was soon seriously wrong.

Work began in the closing weeks of 1980. By April 1981 the bank balance was exhausted. A large bill from Mr Yeung was outstanding. Still confident, Valerie and Wendy took the bill to the chapel and spread it out before their Lord. Many times before they had been taken to the "eleventh hour" before the necessary provision had arrived. Surely it would happen again?

Wendy believes God spoke to her during this period from the Bible: 'We must through many tribulations enter. . .' (Acts 14.22).

"We were beginning to understand the tribulations. The really tremendous word in that verse, though, was the definite 'enter'. I believed God was promising us that eventually the new building would be ours.

"It was also during this time that I read a short article in my devotional readings about a lady sitting at her typewriter when she saw a moth struggling to get out of its cocoon. She helped it out and as a consequence it died."

For her the interpretation of the message was clear: if we try to push things beyond the natural order then there will be death. God had a plan, which they were not to accelerate or it would fail.

"We believed there was to be a huge struggle ahead before we 'entered' the new buildings. Knowing that God had said this meant we could cope. He also reminded me that Abraham himself never entered into the Promised Land. I had to be prepared not to physically enter in, not to see the fulfilment. That would not mean that God had broken his promise. The Bible tells us (Numbers 23:19) that 'God is not a man that he should lie, neither the son of man that he should repent.'

"It was during that same period, speaking at a women's meeting, when I felt the anointing of God on me in such measure as I had never experienced, before or since. I talked of how I was willing for God to stop everything; that I was willing for this whole work to come to nothing if it was to God's glory. I shared how we were experiencing a sense of privilege that God could trust us with all this heartache. Valerie and I really felt we were the most privileged people on earth.

"I remember also reading in the Old Testament about the Year of Jubilee. This was a time when the slave could go free – but if he didn't want to then he could be nailed to the doorpost, as a sign that he wanted to be enslaved to his master for life. That's how I felt about serving Jesus. The experience was so real to me that I almost expected to awake one morning and find there was a hole pierced through my ear," remembers Wendy.

"I was ready for God to take everything. In fact, God was preparing to take from me the one child I would never have wished to be parted from. . ."

But that was yet to come.

By the end of July 1981 nothing in a practical sense had changed, and the awful decision had to be made.

"We didn't understand why – but we had to close the site," says Valerie.

"We couldn't believe it. How exciting it had been that year, seeing the work going on, the site swarming with workers," recalls Wendy.

"If it was just a matter of *us* waiting, well. . . we would have waited longer. But Mr Yeung desperately needed money to pay his workers. Apparently his life had even been threatened because of it. When we heard that, we knew we couldn't put him in jeopardy. So we called a halt to the work. It was one of the hardest things we ever had to do."

On the side of the site office were painted the words "Jesus Christ is Lord". Valerie and Wendy had been so confident that God was going to provide them with a new building for an expanded work with needy children. It wasn't long before the voices of condemnation were heard chattering. Surely the two women had been out of the Lord's will? It was a traumatic time. It wasn't easy to answer the questions or deal with the accusations.

Time passed. Weeds sprang up around the neglected foundations. Eventually the wooden form work rotted and had to be taken down as it was feared unsafe. The site was to remain untouched for more than six long years.

With the virtue of hindsight, is there any explanation?

One practical matter suggests a possible reason why the project might have been shelved for a time by a divine hand.

Some months after the site was closed down, a government plan was announced to build a new public walkway over the road adjacent to the Home. Forty feet of the garden would be claimed by compulsory purchase order. Had building still been in progress at this time it would certainly have been halted then.

Valerie and Wendy lodged a complaint, suggesting that an underpass be built instead of a walkway. But an underpass was dismissed as a potential danger to the public and the government engineer said that there was no way to re-position the proposed walkway.

The reaction from Valerie and Wendy was that God was most certainly able to re-locate it. A day of prayer and fasting was held. Some suggested that it would be better to give in and receive the compensation – possibly millions of dollars. Wouldn't that pay for a new building outright?

But Valerie and Wendy believed that this course of action would not be true to the vision God had given them for a new Home. Scripture verses they read confirmed that God was not only the champion of orphans but also the protector of His own land, which could not be sold or exchanged. At the end of the six months appeal period, they agreed together to make no public protest. They preferred God to work.

The overpass was built further down the road.

Fortunately Mr Yeung's business in no way suffered through the premature closing of the site: the architect was able to recommend him for other jobs until such time as the work recommenced, and he is still working for the Home of Loving Faithfulness to this day.

Eventually the building fund began to receive donations again. But it was not until 1987 that the work was resumed, and this time on only three of the proposed nine units.

In September 1990 – exactly a quarter of a century after Valerie and Wendy had first opened their doors to Hong Kong's severely handicapped – the Home of Loving Faithfulness family moved into the first of their beautiful new units. On that date, Fu Fu and Wing Kit, two of the original three children taken in on the very first day, were among those taking up their new residence.

"We never thought the building plan was a mistake," states Valerie definitely. "Of course, the delays were devastating. But we always knew the plan was God's. Maybe He had more to teach us before we were ready for the new buildings. Lots of people questioned us and it was hard to take their criticism. But we're not responsible for God or for what He does. Naturally, we continually examined ourselves to see if the delays were due to some fault in us. But we didn't come up with an answer."

Yet, while there might have been some criticism, there was also some acclaim. By the 1980s the work in Sheung Shui, small though it was, was gaining a reputation for excellence in the care of the handicapped that reached far beyond the boundaries of Hong Kong. Government departments began to recognise and praise the standard of nursing; there were TV programmes and radio interviews; speaking engagements and fund-raising events. The publicity was something both women found hard to handle. They weren't looking for the limelight. Valerie remembers how uncomfortable she felt when she was nominated for – and won – the $30,000 Zonta Achievement Award for her contribution to local social services.

"There were several candidates, all interviewed by a panel of leading public figures, and then a presentation at an evening dinner. I borrowed an evening dress and felt awful in it. I found the atmosphere so artificial."

HON HEI

Meanwhile, family life continued with all its happy comings and sad goings. Naturally, there was great excitement over the prospect of taking in a new 10-month-old baby boy.

Hon Hei's tiny frame housed a multitude of physical and mental disorders – he was brain damaged through a jaundice infection, had a rare blood disorder, and was epileptic, as well as suffering from a series of unusual allergies. According to his medical notes he was also blind and deaf – but this proved to be wrong.

When Wendy first saw him he was so very pale yellow and insignificant-looking that, wrapped in the hospital linen, he reminded her of a miniature body in grave clothes. His tiny body was wrinkled like an old man's.

"I thought of how it says in the Bible that not even a sparrow falls to the ground without Jesus knowing. He was as tiny as a little bird. So we nicknamed him Robin."

Robin's mother had died of epilepsy and the rest of the family couldn't cope with his frequent chest infections needing long stays in hospital. Certainly he was not easy to nurse. He suffered fits continually.

What joy it was that within a few weeks Robin was

transformed into a gorgeous and responsive baby, who thrived, who yelled for his bottle and for attention, who loved to be played with and cuddled! He began to look so absolutely "normal" and everyone adored him, particularly Pui Yee. But – with all those complications ticking away inside – they knew from the beginning that Robin would not be theirs for long.

"At a year old he was beautiful, with chubby pink skin," describes Valerie. "He would sit in a bouncing chair, generally very happy with life. Though if he gave an angry cry we would run to him because we knew that he was due for another fit."

"We used to greet him with 'Good Morning, Your Royal Highness', which he loved," says Wendy.

"On his second birthday we made him a little crown out of cardboard and silver paper. And a cake in the shape of a purple velvet cushion. Grandma even rang the local radio station and got a request played for him."

He died a month later, perfectly peacefully in his sleep. But it was traumatic for the Home, because he was so greatly loved. Even more harrowing was a police investigation and the debate over the possibility of a post mortem, since he had been a ward of the courts. Thankfully, a post mortem was avoided.

TWENTY

Community Life – Lasting Friendships and some Misunderstandings

The 70s and early 80s saw a number of staff changes at the Home of Loving Faithfulness – comings and goings which all left their impression on the little community.

There was Lai Shim, also known as Irene, who worked for 10 years at the Home before leaving to use her lovely singing voice to tour with the School of Sacred Music. And Sze Man, who came as a young 15-year-old and, now married with two young sons, is still a frequent visitor to the Home. And Annie, who struggled with and overcame the physical demands of the work before leaving for Canada to become companion to an elderly lady. During 1980 a quiet self-contained Chinese girl called Helen came to work at the Home for a fortnight. And quietly stayed on till this day. Dependable and faithful, sweet-natured even in stressful times, she became an important member of the Home of Loving Faithfulness family.

Another excellent Chinese staff member who was at the Home through the 80s was a young girl with the unlikely name of Shadow. Very much a raw recruit when she came, she quickly learned how to care for the children. Her early abrupt manner hid a very low esteem – largely the result of an unhappy home life. Among their repeated criticisms, her family always told her that she would never find a man and get married. But by nature she was a romantic – and it was actually at the Home of Loving Faithfulness that she found the love that led to marriage and happiness. She married Ah Lam, sometime cook at the Home.

A few months after the wedding, held at the Home with much joy and many traditional customs, Shadow and Ah

Lam left to become houseparents to seven handicapped children at a government-subvented family home. But in 1990 Shadow returned to the staff of the Home of Loving Faithfulness while Ah Lam took up a place at Bible College.

With staff shortage a constant battle throughout the history of the Home, volunteers and student helpers have frequently been part of the 'extended family' at Sheung Shui. It was in 1970 that students first came as summer workers from Anderson College in Indiana, USA. The Home provided board and lodging and weekends off for sightseeing in return for their work with the children and in the laundry. Most summers since then have seen two or three American students from Anderson spending up to eight weeks at the Home.

Other students have come from the Scotland-based Project Trust to stay for a longer period. One came as part of the Duke of Edinburgh Award Scheme, several nursing students have come from Holland, and some half a dozen social work students from the Hong Kong Polytechnic.

Although some of the students have brought with them a variety of difficult personal problems, many have been excellent workers, and their sense of fun and youthful enthusiasm has been invigorating for everyone. Most loved the children and readily accepted the different lifestyle, climate, diet and long working hours. Many have maintained links with the Home over the years, and several have gone on to careers with the handicapped. At least one has had a handicapped son of her own – and her joyful, positive response to his arrival was testimony enough of what she had learned in Hong Kong.

Guy was one volunteer who developed a special relationship with the Home. A local Hong Kong Chinese boy, he first visited the Home to sing Christmas carols with a group of college students. He left school and went to work as a teller in a bank. But he couldn't forget the children and became a willing worker at the Home in his free time. He was prepared to do anything. He would sweep up, clean the fans, take Wing Kit or Che Kin for a walk around the garden, even help with the book keeping.

Eventually, and unsurprisingly, Guy decided he wanted to work full-time with the handicapped. He left the bank and worked at the Home while applying for jobs. Later he went on to study medicine in the States.

"For nine years we prayed for him to become a Christian. While he was studying in the States he finally did come to know Jesus as his personal Saviour – and rang us at 4am one morning to tell us all about it!"

In 1982 an English couple in their early 40s arrived to join the work, through contact that Valerie and Wendy had with a large Baptist church in England.

Warm-natured Mary, short, fair and plump, was a trained nurse and quickly fitted in to the daily routine with the children.

Richard's role was to take charge of the transport as well as practical work around the house. One of his first projects was a novel idea for extending the accommodation.

"We had the idea of getting an old railway carriage to make into staff accommodation in the grounds, but when we looked at the details it was going to be too difficult," remembers Valerie.

"But then it was suggested that we have a bus. Kowloon Motor Bus Company said they would donate one and Richard went to choose it. We had to take the fence down to get it into the garden. Once there Richard worked on the conversion with a student volunteer."

It was a great success. With running water and electricity it proved a very practical extension to the Home. Originally intended for voluntary staff or visitors, Pui Yee liked it so much she moved permanently into the upper deck. To everyone's great amusement she stated that she enjoyed walking to work every day! So she lived there happily for many years, crossing the garden the dozen or so paces to the main house, until she was persuaded to move into the first phase of the new building in 1990.

The bus was one of Richard's most successful projects. However, he was the only male staff member, and with two strong, capable women in charge, such as Valerie and Wendy, there were bound to be tensions.

Matters came to a head and Richard and Mary left, moving into a friend's flat nearby, some 20 months after they had come out to Hong Kong.

The two friends felt hurt, confused and misunderstood. They were deeply disappointed over what had happened.

Mei Yee, a young Chinese nurse on the staff, didn't stay long after Mary and Richard left. Happily, she went on to pursue a fine career in hospice work in Hong Kong.

Wendy afterwards believed it had been a basic mistake to take a married couple onto the staff when the calling was not equally felt.

Another sad and hurtful chapter in the life of the Home drew to its conclusion. Human beings are apt to make such a mess of personal relationships sometimes. But, because of God, that was not entirely the end of the story. With time and God's grace came apology, forgiveness, healing, a measure of understanding, and restoration of friendship. Mary and Richard have remained in Hong Kong and now enjoy a fruitful ministry in a Chinese church which they established. Indeed, it was Richard who led the baptism service for Andrew, Wendy's adopted son, when he came to an age of understanding and wanted to make a public declaration of his desire to serve Jesus.

There have been times of great staff shortages, causing Valerie, Wendy and Pui Yee to cry out to God for relief. But they are thankful for the many who have given of their time and energies generously to the Home.

Lee was gratefully taken on just after the newly-weds Shadow and Ah Lam left. After a week's trial she announced she was so exhausted that she didn't feel life at the Home was for her. The lifting seemed too much for her slight frame. But after a few weeks away she was drawn back; she battled to overcome the physical stresses, and has become an invaluable staff member.

Most of the current staff are unmarried and live in. But Ah Ling and Ah Ying are two that have husbands and children of their own and come in daily. Ah Ling first came as a cleaner. Later she asked to work with the children and proved consistent and caring. Ah Ying, the current cook at the Home, is another real asset, being "calm, gentle and uncomplaining" – characteristics so helpful when the number sitting down for any meal can vary tremendously at short notice!

NO FAIRY STORY

All the staff have discovered for themselves that life at the Home of Loving Faithfulness is no fairy story. Not all the endings are "happily ever after". There are the days when the lifting hurts the back, the laundry is unending, a child's sickness is a nagging pain in the heart.

"Sometimes," admits Valerie, "the day seems just drudgery and I could simply run away. When you feel so tired and you have to keep going, generally from 5am through to 9pm, then you feel as if you're in a beautiful prison and you long to get out. I love going out and meeting people. And it's hard not to have much fellowship with other Christians.

"But then I know I wouldn't leave. Because this is where God wants me to be and he's given us so many blessings. There's a lot of happiness as well as heartache.

"And on the good days there's lots of fun and laughter.

Even the hills and trees around the Home give me a lot of joy; and the animals and the beautiful insects. I long to have more time to study God's lovely Creation.

"When I think how God has trusted us with these children – that, too, gives me a lot of joy."

TWENTY-ONE

Daniel and His Many Lions

How do you explain little Chi Sang's arrival into this world? Some might call it a cruel joke. A terrible mistake. A tragedy.

Many of the children at the Home have extreme physical deformities. Yet, the joy of it is that they do not recognise them as such. Being mentally disabled means they are blissfully ignorant of their own appearances. And because Valerie and Wendy and Pui Yee, from hearts of love, can kiss and cuddle and lavish praise on them – what does it matter if their bodies are twisted? Within the security of the Home of Loving Faithfulness their physical limitations and abnormalities are irrelevant.

But Chi Sang. Chi Sang emerged into this world with a normal, thinking, reasoning brain. But he arrived with neither arms nor legs. There was hardly the suggestion of a minute limb bud on his forlorn trunk.

When Wendy heard of his condition, though he was not mentally handicapped and therefore not normally to be considered for the Home, she felt compelled to visit him and to learn all she could about him. His deformity was no thalidomide tragedy, nor the result of any wrong medication. But Wendy came to believe that it was caused by carelessness and confusion over the results of pregnancy tests and subsequent treatment. Twice the young woman's womb was scraped. It must have been then that the secret foetus was interrupted in its development. Amazingly, the head and torso escaped damage and was delivered by Caesarian section at full term.

His parents resigned the limbless baby to hospital care. They are not to be blamed. In a western country the arrival

159

of such a baby would have unleashed a whole barrage of medical care and financial compensation. It's different in Hong Kong. The parents were poor and had no prospects of being any other way. In a community with few facilities for the handicapped, love sometimes suffers at the hands of expediency. Their narrow world knew of no way of coping with a limbless child.

So Chi Sang's world was bounded by the cot bars of the "minimum handling" ward at the hospital. The medical profession didn't know how to cope with him. They tried to place him in a children's home but no one else could cope with him either. His feverish body, with his normal temperature of 39 degrees, presented a major problem. One of the body's natural methods of maintaining its right temperature is by cooling through its limbs. So a limbless body is constantly above temperature and often feverish, with the danger of convulsions.

"He was about 10 months old when I first saw him in hospital," remembers Wendy. "He looked so lost and alone in his cot. He rocked from side to side. He cried a great deal, screamed and shouted frequently and never smiled. Because of his high temperature he was never picked up and held. The only relief from lying in his cot was when he was placed in a little flowerpot thing they had made for him to try to get him upright. They would sit him in it on a table facing the TV in the ward. His trunk was completely encased and he hated it because he got even hotter."

Wendy was horrified to discover that his nickname on the ward was 'Tung Tung' – 'Little Marrow'.

One day, she thought, he would know exactly what a little marrow was. When she talked about him with Valerie they re-named him Daniel – because he would have to face many lions.

Wendy fell in love with him from the start. She couldn't bear him to be in hospital. She longed to love him and to teach him to love life.

But how could he fit into their Home? He would need special stimulus, education, carefully-designed equipment. And his need for emotional counselling was not to be underestimated. His brain was whole, but not healthy and sound. There was some scarring that was deeper than the physical. Later he would shudder and scream inexplicably at certain sounds such as the scraping of a spoon in a bowl. And Wendy and Valerie came to believe that his agony was his recall of the surgeon's scraping, wrenching tool, as he worked in the mother's womb. Their experience with Daniel confirmed in their hearts the sensitivity and awareness of the unborn.

Daniel's helpless body was so tense, so rigid, so seemingly full of anger. His natural reflex was to turn away from people, not towards them.

"If we didn't take him we were committing him to spending the rest of his life rolling in a hospital bed as 'Little Marrow'. He needed so much more than that. If nothing else, we could give him security and love."

They prayed and commenced the inevitable paperwork. Daniel arrived at the Home four days before his first birthday. Wendy began the slow process of re-educating the little boy. The first task was to win his trust with love.

At the beginning he would shut himself right off from her and turn away, which he was able to do surprisingly well because of a lot of movement he had developed in his right shoulder area.

It was as if, even at a year old, Daniel knew enough to be disillusioned with life and with people.

Wendy recalls, "He had a very bad temper. When he got angry he would bang his bottom up and down and scream. Pui Yee and I, who had most care of him, agreed together that we would feed him nothing but love – whatever his reaction.

"And we wanted to feed into him the certainty that God was not to be blamed for the way he had been born."

This was the message that they communicated to him in dozens of ways. God knew about Daniel and had a plan for him just the way he was. In God's eyes Daniel had no missing bits. God had given him special challenges which he would learn to overcome.

After a few weeks Daniel turned away less and less; he watched them carefully with big round soulful eyes, still wary and keeping his distance. They noticed an almost imperceptible relaxing of his body.

The real key that "unlocked" Daniel was a visit from a missionary doctor called Janet. Wendy asked her for ideas for giving the little boy more activity. She had tried tying things around Daniel's head, but he had hated it. Janet suggested utilising the movement and strength in his right shoulder. They taped on a lightweight chopstick with sticking plaster and hung a bell onto the end.

"He rang it and rang it! It really liberated him."

Daniel experienced the joy of successful communication for the first time. Now he was more willing to be helped. Wendy wasn't slow to capitalise on that early breakthrough.

"I lay awake for hours each night thinking of ways to get him through normal development. I made elastic braces with hooks on the shoulders. Into these hooks we could put spoons, brushes, felt tip pens. He learned to paint, to draw beautiful squiggles and circles, to pick up, explore and play with sand and water – the kind of enjoyments ordinary kids had. Eventually, using cup hooks, he could even do jigsaws. And with a nylon tea strainer he could play ball!"

What invention! What joyful, wonderful triumphs! But there was more.

"Using strips of aluminium, a net bag and five wheels, I made him a walker. By tossing his head he could 'walk' all over the playroom. When he first managed it, he threw himself around until he was exhausted, screeching with delight.

"After that we would hang him in a baby bouncer with a stool underneath so that he could feel what it was like to take his weight. We wanted him to learn to balance and to stand by himself on his bottom."

Daniel truly did begin to love life, to love people, and to love the world around him.

"He loved nature – cats, dogs, flowers, trees, butterflies, birds. He would sit watching in the garden for ages, entranced. He loved to be taken outside at night to see the moon."

Speech came slowly and there was tremendous difficulty in teaching him to feed himself, but it was obvious that in all other areas Daniel was making great progress. Mentally there was no way in which he could be defined as retarded. But emotional deprivation for the first year of his life had taken its toll.

They wanted him to learn to be at ease with people – but that was very hard.

"Taking Daniel out was usually a draining experience. We always put him in a baby carrier or a pushchair facing outwards so that he could see a lot. We had to get him used to people staring," says Wendy.

"It would make me angry how insensitive people were. They assumed that because he had no arms and legs he must have no brain. Some giggled in embarrassment. Older people would openly talk and point at him." The staff at the Home were praying for another miracle, asking God for a family to adopt Daniel. Wendy longed to adopt him herself, so dearly did she love him. But she knew that her own future was in Hong Kong and she felt that Daniel's prospects would be brighter living in the States, Canada or England. Overseas there would be special education and the kind of resources and equipment that would truly minimise his handicap.

It was early in 1982 that Wendy first received a letter postmarked San Jose, California. Jim was the single father of several adopted boys with special needs. He had seen a photo of Daniel and wrote to say he would like to adopt him.

"We had very mixed feelings," recalls Wendy. "Of course, we were thrilled that someone wanted to love him. But we felt it would be better if he had a mother as well as a father.

"However, we corresponded with Jim and on Daniel's birthday Jim rang and sent a gift. Jim wrote very positively of his relationship with God. He had polio as a child and spent long periods of time in hospital – which was the start of his concern for handicapped kids."

Valerie and Wendy began to build up a picture of Jim's household. There were two older boys who had left home – one a grown-up foster son, one adopted son who had gone into the Army. At home were four adopted handicapped sons – 16-year-old Jay and three younger ones called Tom, David and Donald. All four boys were out during the day, two of them at the centre where Jim did part-time teaching.

Was this the right family for Daniel? Wendy was naturally anxious. Would the Social Welfare Department give her permission to take him on a visit to Jim's home? In principle there was no objection, but they pointed out the difficulty of getting the necessary papers for Daniel to enter the States. They agreed to back Wendy if she decided to pursue the matter.

Wendy did pursue it. And it wasn't easy.

"During one phone call I made I was asked, 'So, you want to export this child to the United States.' I was so angry! This was a child we were talking about, not a television set.

"I was continually told it was hopeless for me to attempt to get a visa for Daniel. But I persisted. I persisted because I felt God was telling me that Daniel would get that visa – he had already granted it. In faith I went ahead and bought our return tickets.

"But at the first interview the application was turned down. I asked to see someone higher in authority – and again the visa was refused. The consul was away, so I asked to see the vice-consul. I told him plainly that God had already granted Daniel his visa and the American Consulate could not stand against God. The vice-consul said he would consult the rules and regulations again and be in touch."

It was a tense time. Wendy made all the arrangements with the airline for Daniel's special equipment and started packing. Finally it was a week before the departure date and she had heard nothing about his visa. Six days. Five.

Finally, the vice-consul himself rang. A three-week visa had been granted on humanitarian grounds.

It was a difficult flight, with Daniel fretful, unable to sleep and refusing to eat.

And what did Wendy think of Jim and the home he was offering her beloved Daniel?

"He was one of the nicest men I had ever met. Very genuine. Very caring and accepting. And the boys were great – I got on especially well with David."

Yet Wendy felt anxious that Jim was doing too much and would not be able to give attention to Daniel's very demanding needs. Another thing that worried her was the standard of everyday hygiene in the hectic all-male household. After all, Daniel spent a lot of time on the floor. Jim's mother, too, was of the opinion that Jim had taken on a great deal with his present family and didn't always take proper care of himself. At the end of the stay both Wendy and Jim agreed that this was not the right place for Daniel.

The time in California, though, was very useful for making contacts. Wendy was able to visit a specialist in limb deficient children. And Jim himself was established as a good friend. Later that year Wendy was able to take advantage of a free air ticket to travel to the States again to visit a specialist company about equipment tailor-made for Daniel, using Jim's home and his contacts.

"In New York I collected an automatic feeding machine we wanted to try with Daniel, spent the night in the airport and then flew on to California where Jim had found someone we hoped could make an electric wheelchair for him.

"I took with me a plaster cast of Daniel's body. The modifications for his limbless body would cost more than the actual wheelchair. But we didn't hesitate over the cost – we felt Daniel really needed it. The seat was a floating plate on a spring with four pressure buttons to control the direction of the movement."

Daniel, at first very frightened of the wheelchair, grew in confidence and found his new freedom wonderful.

Then came a letter from Gina and Ray of Canada. Like Jim, they were parents of adopted children with special needs – not so unusual in the States and Canada, where there is a comprehensive support and welfare system for such families. This couple, though, had no fewer than 15 children.

Only one son, John, was their natural child. Five children were from an Indian family: their father had been an alcoholic and the mother had committed suicide. Then there was Chrissie, an adopted black girl, full of life and energy, aged about 12. Doreen had spina bifida. Ticey from Vietnam was a hyperactive child with intense emotional problems. A Canadian Chinese boy, David, suffered from failing sight. Linda was a large 11-year-old with low intelligence who had previously been in nine or ten different foster homes. Joshua was limb deficient. Patrick was diagnosed as psychotic – there was nothing organically wrong with him but his behaviour was difficult and erratic. Tali, the youngest at three years old and a special favourite of Ray, was an extremely bright Jewish girl with limb deficiencies – she had stumps for arms and short legs with no knees.

Gina and Ray, as parents of this amazing family, had won several awards in recognition of their achievements, and were much in demand as speakers at adoption conferences.

Having seen his details on an internationally-circulated list of hard-to-place children, they wanted Daniel to be their sixteenth child. After a visit to the family in May 1983, Wendy was unsure.

"I knew I couldn't really be objective, because I loved Daniel so much and, of course, I wanted everything to be perfect for him. There was a lot that was positive. Gina and Ray really loved their children and were committed to them."

Gina, whose dark hair, high cheekbones and extrovert personality betrayed her Italian blood, was very much the driving force in the family, Wendy decided.

"But Ray, heavily built and with already greying hair, was far from being the henpecked husband. He could be firm. But he was also very sensitive to the children. Their marriage seemed very strong. They were both very accepting people. With so much acclaim it was hard to criticise them.

"I knew I really had to let Daniel go. Common sense told me that Hong Kong was not the place for him to have his needs met. I wanted him to have a mother and father whom he could love. Ultimately it would not be my decision, anyway, but the Adoption Unit's."

So why did Wendy have reservations about Gina and Ray? Mostly because Daniel was going to be their sixteenth child. Because Ray and Gina were not committed Christians but nominal Catholics. And because she felt that they were very casual about the special appliances of the other handicapped children in the family.

"I was worried that they didn't care much about making sure these children were wearing their special arms and legs. If no one bothered to give Daniel his artificial limbs when he got them, then he might as well be in Hong Kong. That kind of deprivation would be terrible for him."

In spite of her apprehensions, the Adoption Unit approved Ray and Gina's application. But in fact it was August 1984 before Daniel left for Canada because of the need for ministerial approval.

During the intervening nine or ten months Wendy did her best to prepare Daniel for his new life. She asked his new family for a cassette tape of all their voices, and she continually played the messages and songs over to him, until he would get excited and sing along with little Tali.

The time for parting at last drew near. Wendy escorted Daniel to Canada and stayed for two weeks, gradually weaning him off his dependence on her. It seemed as if Daniel would cope. But Wendy was in turmoil. The prospect of leaving Daniel was agonising. She didn't hand over Daniel's passport to Ray and Gina for days, rehearsing an improbable scene in her imagination in which she grabbed Daniel and ran away with him. The goodbyes were unbearable.

She didn't see him again till the following April. Contact by letter and phone communicated that all was well and Wendy's fears for the little boy subsided, though the love and longing for him remained. Then Gina suggested a visit and Wendy got a cheap courier flight to San Francisco and on to Toronto.

"Daniel was in the house when I arrived. There he was, a little five-year-old standing in the doorway, with his legs strapped on and his protective crash helmet, just home from school. He simply couldn't take in the fact that I was there."

Wendy soon saw that he was grieving. She began to discover things that made her sick at heart. Apparently it had been months in his new home before he'd said a word. Gone was the loud singing and happy talk that she remembered. She noticed that he was rocking himself to sleep – something she well recalled from his early days at Sheung Shui. She found that he spent a lot of time without other children at home, unattended. It wasn't deliberate neglect. But there were a lot of legitimate things to be done to care for so many children – shopping, laundry, visits to doctors and dentists and so on.

Wendy's heart was full as she sensed Daniel's hurts. And she wasn't able to leave without voicing her criticism in strong terms. It caused a dramatic rift between her and the family. After her return to Hong Kong, Gina wrote asking Wendy not to communicate with them any more and to stop sending letters and gifts for Daniel. She said that his grief after Wendy had left had broken their hearts.

Wendy's fragile heart was broken, too. Devastated, she communicated her concerns about Daniel's placement to the Social Welfare Department. She wanted Daniel back in Hong Kong. With her. It was a thought that obsessed her. Unfortunately perhaps, the direct outcome of Wendy's action was the sending of someone from Canadian social services to investigate the problems. It caused a further barrier between her and Gina and Ray. The professional opinion was that more time was needed for the bonding of Daniel and his family and all would be well.

Wendy knew in her heart that she had caused a lot of trouble for the family. Her only consolation was that she believed they knew that she had been motivated by just one thing. Love for Daniel.

"After all this I was so depressed," admits Wendy. "It was the closest I ever came to losing my faith or to suicide. I put myself on night duty for weeks so that I wouldn't have to face anyone, not even Valerie or the other staff. For months I was tortured in my imagination as to what Daniel was facing. I couldn't talk about it to anyone."

Wendy, Valerie and Pui Yee continue to pray for Daniel by name every day, as they do for all their adopted children. Brief contact over the years has communicated that he is doing well with his artificial limbs – special lightweight legs and myoelectric arms which respond to stimulus from his muscles, though in 1990 he went through real medical problems. At the Home they pray that all is well with his soul. Thankfully, the relationship with Gina and Ray has greatly improved and the letters exchanged these days are warm and loving.

"When I'm really tired," says Wendy, "I think 'Wouldn't Daniel love to have legs to run up and down these stairs; wouldn't he love to have arms to carry this load of washing!'" Wendy writes him a postcard every month. She doesn't know if he receives it. Still, she thinks of him continually.

TWENTY-TWO

The Oldest Arrival – and Two More Young Ones

In 1981, the same year that the tiny limbless Daniel came to be the youngest member of the Home of Loving Faithfulness family, one more new arrival came as the oldest – and possibly the most entertaining.

Grace was approaching 44 years old. When she was born in 1938 with Downs syndrome, the daughter of a relatively well-off Chinese family living in the UK, her condition was viewed very negatively. The family were told that she would be "nothing but a vegetable". No help or training was offered.

Yet the family, who were Christians, found it difficult to accept the gloomy prognosis. They wondered if there was something that could be done medically. They returned to Hong Kong, intending to take Grace into China to pursue treatment with traditional herbal medicines.

However, they were overtaken by history. With the outbreak of war in Hong Kong they were forced to remain there.

Little Grace grew up in the safety of the family home, never seeing anything of life outside those protective walls. In fact, many of the family's friends didn't even know of her existence. And she would have continued to remain something of a secret but for the need for dental treatment when she was about 12 years old. Grace strongly resisted any attempt to persuade her to leave the house, so help was sought from a missionary clinic to treat her at home.

Generally Grace was amiable enough, could walk and feed herself after a fashion, and the family coped well with her. As the years passed a son emigrated to the United

States, married and children were born. Other members of the family emigrated, too. But the parents, now getting older, were prevented from joining them because of Grace. Their longing to be with their children and grandchildren grew. Father had residential status for the States, but mother could never stay long enough to be granted it as she was needed in Hong Kong for Grace. Attempts to get permission to take Grace to the States failed.

Valerie and Wendy first heard of the family through an English missionary working with the same dental and medical clinic that had been caring for Grace over several decades. The family attended the church fellowship attached to the clinic.

Could the Home of Loving Faithfulness take Grace in to free the parents to join the rest of their family overseas? The parents would not consider Grace being admitted to a non-Christian institution.

"I did visit the family, and they pleaded with me to take her," says Wendy. "But at that time we had no place for Grace, and the need was not so urgent. She was not putting any physical strain on them, although she was tremendously overweight. She loved cakes and all sweet things and they gave them to her generously to keep her happy."

But a couple of years later the situation had altered. The ageing mother was bowing to pressure from the rest of the family to leave for the States. The plan was to leave Grace in the care of an *amah*, who was herself in her sixties. The family home would be let out, with Grace and the *amah* living in rooms on the roof – a not uncommon Hong Kong scenario. The prospect worried Valerie and Wendy. What if the *amah* was unreliable or got sick? What if a fire broke out?

Then Chan Mei left the family for a full-time place at a training centre. Her bed was in a small room which she shared with the Home's talkative skateboarder, Fung Tai.

That room was suitable only for a more able handicapped person – and the only one on their list who qualified was Grace. The timing of this convinced them that it was right to admit her. As with Sau Ming, they saw this as a need to help a "household of faith".

"We were absolutely amazed at how well she reacted to the change," recalls Valerie, remembering the arrival of the short, very plump Grace with her hair cut drastically above her ears. "She was used to spending every day on her own, with just an *amah* to care for her. Now she was in a large community."

Valerie and Wendy put her on a strict diet to lose some of those unnecessary pounds. "We deprived her of sweets, chocolates and other sugary things, though the first Easter we did let her have a chocolate egg. How she gorged herself!" says Wendy.

"We had a few tussles with her at first because she was so strong. If she didn't want to move, it would take three of us to get her along the corridor, struggling and wriggling."

Grace was an expert at furniture moving – shoving unwanted items from her room out onto the balcony.

In preparation for her arrival, the room she was to share with Fung Tai had been given a thorough spring clean and made pretty with frilled curtains in pink and white gingham, matching bedspreads on new truckle-beds, new white kidney-shaped dressing tables, easy chairs and a small table. The room was not to remain long in its pristine order. As soon as the wind blew the curtains, Grace rushed at them, tore them into pieces and threw the shreds onto the balcony. Even the curtain rails came down. In her first few weeks she continually ransacked the drawers. Visitors would be entertained by the sight of items of underwear lined up on her bed. The beds, which Grace used as springboards, had to be changed, and the dainty dressing tables substituted with a lockable cupboard – though it was found that she could even move that around the room and it would often be found blocking the doorway or pushed outside. Posters were ripped from walls, formica tops were peeled away. Gradually, of necessity, the room became more and more spartan. It was tempting to assign her to a mattress in the corridor!

Poor Fung Tai, her roommate, tried endlessly to establish a relationship by giving her small toys to hold. These were all unceremoniously thrown into the corner.

One vital piece of equipment which arrived at the Home with Grace was her rattan waste paper basket. This was filled with empty plastic film cartridges and a few toys. The film cases constituted one of her many obsessions – like the underwear, they had to be frequently arranged and re-arranged in meticulous order. Valerie and Wendy used her attachment to this rattan basket to encourage her to move when needed – carrying that from room to room with Grace following proved a lot easier than carrying Grace! Over time, the plastic cases were replaced with small toys and the rattan bin with a more hygienic washable plastic laundry basket.

Grace's suitcase from home contained the most awful shapeless clothes imaginable. These mainly consisted of tops which were simply two straight pieces of material sewn together at the sides and shoulders. Valerie and Wendy soon had some appreciation of the reason for this depressing wardrobe. Any nice new clothes Grace was given she would remove at the earliest opportunity. Failing that, she would systematically remove all the buttons.

Eventually the women learned to sew up all button openings on Grace's clothes whenever possible. After a battle or two she would accept T-shirts and shorts, or track suits and jumpers in the winter. But the possibility of an impromptu striptease at any time or in any place has remained one of the lively features of Grace's character, and, given a chance and being something of an aimless wanderer, she is always likely to try absconding. When determined she can put on an amazing burst of speed, even though she's now in her fifties.

TWENTY YEARS ON

Following Grace's admission in 1981 there was stability in terms of numbers in spite of some instability in the staffing of the Home. No new children were taken in for over four years, though there were four departures during this period – the deaths of Mei Ling and Siu Kuen and the adoptions of Ross and Daniel, which altogether reduced the numbers to 15.

By the summer of 1985 – some 20 years after Valerie and Wendy opened the Home – many of the family were "growing up" in years, though not, of course, maturing in any normal sense of the words. Grace was the oldest at 47, but there were three others in their 30s – Fung Tai (35), Sau Ming (32) and Laan Chan (30). Ngan Ying was now 28, Wing Kit 26, Fu Fu, Shaan Shaan and Lo Shan all 25. Siu Ping, Chi Kin, and Dibs were all teenagers and Wai Man about to have his thirteenth birthday. Wendy's adopted son Andrew was 22, Valerie's daughter Charlotte 11.

That year Wing Kit was seriously ill with a gastric ulcer, but with him recovered and the staff situation calmer, Valerie and Wendy planned to take in two more children.

SIN YEE

Another Downs syndrome child was referred to them, an illegitimate girl aged a year and a half. She had spent her life in various hospital wards, ill much of the time with fairly minor complaints such as urinary tract infections. Valerie and Wendy agreed to take her and began to pray for a family to adopt her. Sin Yee was small for her age, but a cute child with lots of potential. With love and attention she developed quickly and within months of being at the Home she stood and took her first steps. Her first word was "Dadow" for Shadow, the Chinese staff member, and after that she was soon chanting nursery rhymes.

Discovering that Hong Kong's Matilda Child Development Centre sent someone into the New Territories once a week to work with retarded children, Valerie and Wendy dispatched Sin Yee for an assessment and then for weekly sessions. After an unco-operative start she made great progress, so much so that it was felt she would benefit from much more stimulus. Arrangements were made to take her to the morning sessions at the Matilda Hospital special needs unit on Hong Kong Island – no small commitment because it was a tediously long journey during a period of staff shortage. An American student, Jack, who arrived to work as a volunteer for three months, had little time for anything but being Sin Yee's chauffeur. Then another volunteer, an occupational therapist called Teresa, took over the driving. It was this experience with Sin Yee that persuaded Valerie and Wendy to take on a full-time driver and handyman, Kim, who took over the driving schedule.

Kim, who had previously been working for the Salvation Army in Hong Kong, proved a great asset to the Home. And he had a natural feeling for the children. Though his family lived locally, Kim had spent much of his early life in England, where he had met and married an English girl, Deana. The second of the couple's four children was born mentally handicapped.

With Kim to drive Sin Yee over to Hong Kong Island and back every day, a lot of pressure was taken off the family's daily routine needs. And Sin Yee flourished with the special attention. "She had an outgoing personality, which the Matilda unit encouraged," says Valerie. "She was very much a little actress, lively and active and a terrific climber. She fell out of her cot twice and we had to resort to letting her sleep on a mattress on the floor. She loved her food and ate in the dining room with the staff."

One day there was an emotional phone call from a

woman called Suzie who had visited the Home some months previously. She asked if they still had the little girl called Sin Yee, and said she was convinced that God wanted her to adopt the child.

Wendy had reservations when she met the couple. Suzie was a bubbly Sri Lankan, her husband David a quiet Englishman quite a bit older than her, who worked for a French bank. They had one daughter, Priya.

At first Sin Yee seemed to find it difficult to take to Suzie, but as Suzie persisted, slowly Sin Yee's resistance began to give way, along with any doubts that Valerie and Wendy had. The adoption progressed, although not without the usual hold-ups. It was completed in February 1988 and the following month the family went to England at the expiration of their contract. David decided to leave banking and the couple opened a small guest house on the Isle of Wight. Cindy, as she is now named, happily attends a normal school there and is doing well, although she will probably go to a special school in time.

SHUK FUNG

Mrs Cheung's five children by her first marriage were all doing well, all growing fast, with the youngest already in his teens. The neighbours found it hard to understand what prompted her to take an illiterate labourer for her second husband. Superstitiously, they concluded that it was hardly surprising that their baby was born so severely retarded. The little girl was kept in a cot pushed under a shelf unit in a passageway, out of the way of the half-brothers and -sisters who totally rejected her. Mrs Cheung herself had little feeling for the wretched child.

"She just won't feed," she complained repeatedly when Wendy visited the family in their resettlement flat in Tsuen Mun.

That proved quite an understatement. Shuk Fung was

then four years old and weighed eleven pounds and four ounces.

Medical notes revealed that Shuk Fung's condition — severely brain damaged, microcephalic, epileptic and blind — was in fact due to a dormant infection carried by the mother, known as C.M.V. (Cytomegalovirus)

Shuk Fung was admitted to the Home of Loving Faithfulness in October 1985. Apart from her tiny size, two other factors made her a difficult child to handle. One was the bed sore on her back. And the other was the congenital dislocation of both hips which made her legs permanently "frogged" in position. A hip operation had been performed but had achieved nothing since the necessary regular physiotherapy had not been given.

"We couldn't believe how small she was," recalls Wendy. "She came wearing a terrible dark coloured T-shirt and shorts. She was quite dark-skinned and looked an ugly little thing. We washed her straight away, dressed her sore and put her in some new light-coloured clothes."

"We lay her on her tummy to heal the bed sore — which was gone within three weeks — and we really cosseted her," says Valerie.

The mother had fed her by bottle, but Shuk Fung would rarely take more than two ounces at a time.

"I marvelled she was still living. She would only bite the teat when we offered her a bottle, so we put milk in a little medicine cup and she began to drink from that. Soon we were able to feed her small amounts of solids by spoon. And she loved fruit juice."

Quite often Valerie and Wendy felt very moved by the circumstances of the families they met and were drawn to help them.

"But there was nothing in me that responded to this family, even though I knew a lot of their treatment of Shuk Fung came from ignorance. The mother only visited twice. She noticed straight away that Shuk Fung was putting on some weight and that her hair was beginning to grow. But she wasn't really interested in the child."

Splints were made for Shuk Fung's retracted hands and legs and some physiotherapy tried. A nurse from Holland doing three months' voluntary work at the Home worked intensively with her. Sometimes she could be gently lowered into a small paddling pool where she enjoyed splashing about. She smiled more and more and responded well to music.

However, as time passed and in spite of extra attention, her hip and leg distortions made it more difficult for her to be held and her fits became more frequent. Staff noticed that her body temperature was often very low. At first it was assumed that this was shock resulting from a spontaneous fracture of her leg. She became quieter and quieter, and feeding became more and more difficult, requiring great patience, until eventually there was no alternative but to tube feed her. A doctor warned the staff that Shuk Fung's body was slowly but inevitably "slowing down". She died peacefully in December 1989, aged eight. Richard and Mary came to take the funeral service and she was buried on the little hill overlooking the Home.

TWENTY-THREE

Love for Thomas the Unwelcome Twin

Tat Wing and Tat Ming were born to Mrs Yu in January 1983. Perfect identical twin sons. Strangely enough, not both were perfect in Mrs Yu's eyes. Inexplicably, while she lavished her mother's love on Tat Wing, her feelings for Tat Ming were those of rejection. Somehow, the younger twin was unwelcome, unwanted.

How much she struggled against her unloving feelings for Tat Ming is not known. That she felt she needed help was clear from the appeal she made to the organisation Against Child Abuse. After counselling she was sent home – back to her twins. A relative took over some of the daily care of Tat Ming, but only temporarily.

Staff at the day nursery couldn't fail to notice the difference between the upbringing of their two little charges. Tat Wing was content, well fed and nicely clothed. Even spoilt. Tat Ming was undernourished, fearful and sometimes bruised.

The terrible climax to all this occurred one April day in the Yu home. The twins were just over three years old. Tat Ming had a fever and his mother was cross and impatient with him. Reaching for the medicine from the refrigerator she carelessly poured some into the boy's mouth. It was the wrong bottle. It contained her addict husband's maintenance drug, methadone.

Tat Ming was choking and screaming hysterically. Mr Yu gripped his head and began to force water down his throat. It was a scene of utter confusion. It seems likely that it was a combination of the trauma of the incident together with the effects of the drug that sent Tat Ming into cardiac arrest. When the ambulance men arrived, no one could say how long he had not been breathing. However, he was rushed to hospital and resuscitated.

Within a few days Tat Ming emerged from a coma and some measurement of the damage was possible. The cardiac arrest had resulted in brain damage of extreme severity. He was robbed of his sight, speech and motor control. His limbs were stiff, his whole body permanently tense; he was subject to repeated epileptic fits and bouts of terrified crying and screaming.

At last realising the extent of the family problems, the social worker resisted any suggestion of sending Tat Ming home. But when his condition stabilised there was nowhere appropriate to send him. He was put into an out-of-the-way old people's home where there happened to be a spare bed in a tiny upstairs room.

"When I first saw him," recalls Wendy, "he was lying in a large bed covered in a baby quilt. The superintendent of the home agreed that he shouldn't be there, but said that there was no alternative.

"Apparently he was normally crying and distressed, but they had been keeping him on tranquillisers, so that day he was very quiet. He was a very beautiful child."

He was indeed breathtakingly beautiful. It was a point on which everyone who saw him agreed. Flawless skin, a round cherub's face, a high intelligent forehead, large eyes with long lashes, and a full, shapely mouth. He had a thick head of hair which grew straight and strong from his scalp at right angles, like a soft black brush.

Valerie and Wendy agreed immediately that they would take him. He arrived at the Home of Loving Faithfulness in December 1986.

Tat Ming was the first retarded child they had admitted who had experienced some years of normal mental faculties. They began to pray that God would restore to him all he had so tragically lost. And they prayed that God would wipe out all his painful memories.

"We were soon very sure that not all of his memory and understanding were lost. We were convinced that he remembered things from before the accident and much of what had happened to him the day he choked.

"Firstly, there was the way he reacted when we tried to feed him – he would scream, go rigid and vomit. He was re-living the trauma of his choking.

"Then, there was his response when we called his name. He would stiffen and become terrified. We were sure he remembered his mother calling him; and he remembered that when his mother called him he was always in trouble.

"We felt it was very important that he should begin a new life with us. Normally we make every effort to maintain a child's links with his family. But this was different. We wanted to cut him off from his family, to erase his past. We believed that love would give us a breakthrough with him."

He was a little boy full of doubts, so they gave him the new name Thomas, to which he quickly responded. Every mealtime was preceded by prayer, and many different approaches were tried to get Thomas to take liquidised food. For weeks his response was screaming and fear.

A special morning of prayer was held for him in the chapel, attended by staff and volunteer workers.

"Edna, one of the volunteer workers, was holding him in her arms," says Wendy. "We were praying for the healing of his memories of fear and rejection. Edna suddenly felt that his weight was lifted out of her arms, that he weighed nothing."

They took it as a sign of answered prayer, and recorded significant improvements in him from that day on. The first day they saw him smile was wonderful. The effect of his smile was magical. The smile spread slowly until it lit up his whole face – even his unseeing eyes. Then, bit by bit, they managed to get through a whole feed with him not screaming and even reasonably relaxed.

On his fourth birthday Wendy made him a cake with his name on it and they propped him up in a chair. He seemed genuinely happy. With such improvements, they decided to give him physiotherapy. Lack of use had wasted the muscles on his limbs and there was also some twisting of feet and fingers. Grandma went to the hospital to learn from the physiotherapists so that she could repeat the exercises with him daily. A special chair was made for him with a head support and restraints to straighten his arms and legs. His head control showed signs of strengthening. Physically there was no reason why he should not regain the use of his limbs. The staff prayed and worked to that end.

After almost two years at the Home, the hospital ortho-paedic specialist suggested surgery to correct partial dislocation of Tom's hips and contractions of his ankles. It was a fairly routine surgery but would involve the boy being in a plaster cast from his chest downwards for six weeks.

Generally, there was always agreement among Valerie, Wendy and Pui Yee as to treatment for their children. But, for the first time, there was some disagreement as to what was best for Thomas.

Pui Yee, the professional nurse, was keen to go ahead with the surgery. Valerie was hesitant. Wendy fought within herself. She really didn't want him to go into hospital, for past experiences had given her little confidence in the ability of a government hospital to deal with the needs of a retarded child. Yet she didn't want to stand in the way of anything that might improve the child's quality of life.

The appointment card from the hospital arrived in the post. Thomas was to be admitted for surgery in January 1989. But still there was no accord between the three. They met to settle the issue, all putting their views. Pui Yee was for the surgery, but Valerie wasn't at all happy about it. Wendy wasn't sure. Her view was that Tom was going to have a lot of discomfort, and also after the surgery a lot of physiotherapy would be necessary to maintain anything that had been achieved. If they couldn't maintain it because of shortage of staff then the whole thing would have been a waste of time and unnecessary trauma to Tom. But her chief doubts were about the nursing care during the six weeks that Tom would be in hospital.

Wendy had a long talk with the specialist at the hospital. He assured her that the staff were used to handling handicapped children. Yes, he understood that Tom would need turning every hour, night and day, and that two staff members would need to be there to do it.

Wendy slowly came around to agreeing, although her heart was not really in it. She gave explicit details of Tom's condition to the ward staff, including the instruction that he should never be placed in the prone position – lying on his front – due to the frequency of his fits. A young girl who had worked as a volunteer at the Home was now working at the same hospital and promised she would check on Thomas every day.

The operation was a complete success. Back in the ward, in his plaster cast, Tom was obviously not as responsive as he had been, and it was clear that he was missing his Home of Loving Faithfulness family. Staff and volunteer workers visited daily, sometimes twice a day. They took in his favourite musical toys and hung them from the cot side, talked to him reassuringly, fed and changed him.

Three weeks in the plaster cast and all seemed well. Tom celebrated his sixth birthday on the ward immediately before Chinese New Year. Wendy was anxious about the ward being short of staff over the holiday weekend. She wondered about asking for Tom to be released early – she was sure they themselves could cope with the cast – but was so busy herself that she didn't get a chance to speak to the surgeon in charge of his case.

On the Monday morning of the holiday weekend, the phone rang. A voice asked Wendy to come immediately to the hospital.

"There has been an emergency. . . A cardiac arrest. . ."

Wendy could barely find words to tell Valerie what had happened. Overcome with dread and sick at heart, she dared not risk driving into Shatin, so ran out onto the main Sheung Shui road and hailed a taxi.

"Tom's bed had been pushed out into the middle of the ward and they had put an airway into him. They were about to take him to Intensive Care. Twice they asked me to wait outside but I wasn't going to leave him, and when they wheeled him out I followed," recalls Wendy.

She and the volunteer worker Edna were prevented, though, from going into the Intensive Care room. They waited outside in tears, next to the black plastic sack that contained all his birthday presents, toys and equipment, hastily bundled together and brought with him from the ward.

Eventually they were allowed to see him. His body was dwarfed by the banks of monitors and machines of the life support system that was now breathing for him.

They were told that a nurse who went to turn him had discovered that his colour had dramatically changed and that he had no pulse.

Questioning further, though the doctor was insistent Thomas was always correctly positioned, they reached the conclusion that the unthinkable had happened. It seemed as though Thomas had been left prone, not safely on his side. Wendy assumed that he had had a fit, which caused a movement of his head. Then face downward on the white sheets, he had no ability to lift his head himself.

She felt the doctor had lied to protect his staff. There was no internal obstruction to his breathing, as an X-ray showed. Therefore the obstruction had to be external, concluded Wendy.

Wendy couldn't bear to imagine Thomas's trauma and anguish. To be once choked and twice suffocated. . . And

185

if he did survive he would be even more brain damaged than previously.

There was little hope. Valerie, Pui Yee, Wendy, various volunteers – all maintained short vigils by the bedside when permitted. They talked to him and played his favourite tapes.

"But after three days," Wendy recalls, "I was one hundred per cent certain that his spirit had gone from his body, even though he was still breathing because of the machines. I believed Tom was with the Lord. Valerie and Pui Yee felt the same, and so did others who went in to see him.

"That evening we requested that the machines be turned off. The doctor said it was premature because not enough time had elapsed since the giving of anti-convulsant drugs to ensure a diagnosis of brain death.

"From then on it was hard to sit besides him. We felt like hypocrites. We believed Tom had gone and there was no point in watching by his earthly house. But if we stopped visiting, then the message to the hospital would be that we no longer cared, that we had washed our hands of him.

"Still no one admitted that he had suffocated – but most people seemed to know what had happened. While Tom was on the machine we could do or say nothing. We knew that any indication from us that we knew he had suffocated would mean they would fight to keep him 'alive'."

On Sunday evening the ventilator was turned off. And still Thomas kept on "breathing". Wendy describes the next few hours as "a horror story".

"I started to think of all the things I had heard about people saying they had been to Heaven and been brought back again. Were they going to force his spirit back into his body? My theology was totally confused. The next day I asked the doctor what was happening. He said they couldn't prove that Tom was brain dead. He said that his throat had collapsed but the airway could not be left indefinitely before getting infected. They wanted to do a tracheostomy, which might prolong life for three or four months.

"My response was to refuse permission for surgery. I felt that this was their way of avoiding having to say that he had died of suffocation. This way they could say that death resulted from surgery. I begged him to turn all the machines off."

However, ultimately that was unnecessary. Back at the bedside that afternoon, Valerie and Wendy noticed the responses on the monitors were fading, which they saw as an answer to prayer. Valerie stayed on until every flicker had failed, and the hospital admitted that he was really beyond recall.

It was a devastating time. The phone hardly stopped ringing – so many who loved Tom were calling to know what had happened.

"We appeared very diffident in answering people. It was hard to know what to say and it seemed that we didn't care. But we were all worried that if we spoke honestly we would be charged with libelling the hospital."

Tom was buried on the hill overlooking the Home, alongside the other children who had left for a better destination. The death certificate recorded the cause of death as hypoxia – lack of air. Wendy wrote to the hospital asking for a report, following advice from a Crown Counsel friend. The hospital disclaimed negligence. To take things further would have required an autopsy. But after the trauma of his little life, it was decided to let him rest in peace.

One of the many who knew and loved Thomas wrote these words. They were, she said, a kind of epitaph:

Whole and at Home

Two days only since they laid you in the Spring earth.
Four since your last little breath and stammering
   heartbeat.
The see-saw of my emotions still threatens.
Now the tears start to my eyes.
Now the smile springs to my lips.

Thomas, your world here was confined to six years
   and six days.
A mean span of life for so much pain.
Limited cruelly to a cot, your body was a prison.
We struggled to unlock the doors and break through
   the bars.
Longing, we prayed for your big brown eyes to see us;
For your wasted limbs to swell with strength.
Your smile of recognition teased us
With the hope of reaching inside your damaged head
   and heart.

Before the end a beautiful dream picture of your
   destination,
Your new world,
Haunted me sleeping and waking.

Alone, yet not alone,
You ran through a field of tall grass
That bowed before you under a wild, warm summer
   breeze.
You bubbled with joy at the exultation,
The celebration of your whole, perfect body.
Your eyes were alight.
You threw back your head
And I felt again

Love for Thomas the Unwelcome Twin

The touch of that thick black hair standing hedgehog-
   short.
Your smile widened to a grin,
The grin grew to a yell of wordless inexpressible
   delight.
Whole and at home,
Restored,
You raised your arms as you ran,
Saluting both sun and Son.

We longed to set you free.
And now you are.
Gloriously, radiantly free.
Forgive us our sometimes tears.
We miss you.
Now are we the handicapped.
Wait for us.
We're coming.

TWENTY-FOUR

Hard Questions on Healing
and True Value

Valerie, Wendy, Pui Yee and others had prayed for Thomas's healing. But it hadn't happened – at least not in the way they had envisaged. There had been, instead, the greater healing of death.

But if they really believe in an all-powerful, prayer-answering God, do they pray for healing for *all* their children?

"We do believe in prayer and have particular times of prayer in the chapel for specific needs. When the children are ill the chapel is the special place to which we take them," says Wendy.

"But the healing we ask for our children is never for their restoration to full mental understanding."

Isn't this a lack of faith? Wendy answers, "I'm not convinced that any severely mentally handicapped child has ever been miraculously healed. I've never heard of a case of someone brain damaged from birth being healed.

"God is sovereign. I feel very definitely that if God healed a child with brain damage then presumably that child would have to come to the place of accepting or rejecting Him – whereas, before, he or she was already his.

"So, while I would not choose for a child to be born handicapped, spiritually it's 'safer' that they stay the way they are. Our concern for our children is more for their souls than their bodies."

But the case of a person becoming mentally handicapped after being born "normal" is different, Wendy believes.

"Thomas was different, because he was over three years

190

old when he was brain damaged. We believed that God could and would restore him."

For Valerie, the biggest challenge is knowing how to pray when a child becomes ill.

"How should we pray? That the child recovers from his illness and continues in his limited life with his handicaps? Or that he dies and goes to be with the Lord and be perfect?

"When a child dies it's like losing part of your own flesh – but you rejoice that he is with God."

KA YEE

While in Western cultures the unmarried mother is now an accepted part of the community at large, hardly warranting a raised eyebrow, the same easy attitude does not prevail in the East, not even in westernised Hong Kong.

Woon Yi, 22 and single, was urged by her family to have an abortion. It was a simple matter: an hour's train ride over the border into China and there would be a "clinic" to be found on any Shenzhen back street that would deal with the problem cheaply. It was what everyone else did. And no one need ever know.

Woon Yi resisted. Deep down she had a vague feeling that it would be wrong to terminate the little life inside her. She and the father of the baby hastily married and moved in with his mother.

In the family's eyes the birth of the baby girl at Christmas-time 1986 was surely ill-omened. That morning the sister of the mother-to-be died of cancer after a terrible illness. And when little Ka Yee emerged from her mother's womb it was immediately apparent that she was horribly handicapped.

Severely retarded, microcephalic, blind, epileptic, hyperactive and (it was discovered later) suffering from nephrotic syndrome – a condition inhibiting the proper working of the kidneys – the diagnosis must have seemed a curse on the young girl who had insisted on carrying her baby full term. It was discovered that the mother was a carrier of the virus known as C.M.V., the same virus that had given Shuk Fung such handicaps.

A medical social worker referred the case of little Ka Yee to Valerie and Wendy at the Home of Loving Faithfulness and in August they collected her from the Tsuen Wan hospital where she had lived for most of her seven and a half months. Both mother and father had continued to visit their little baby. They lacked the courage to tell most of their friends the truth about Ka Yee – they just said that she was very ill.

Tiny Ka Yee needed much careful nursing. Because of her extreme hyperactivity she needed sedating to give her an hour or two of undisturbed sleep, free from her wild thrashing. She was tube fed and constantly vomited. Admitting her put the short-staffed Home under a tremendous strain. Pui Yee took on much of the constant care vital to the baby and she grew particularly attached to her.

"To look at, she was such a funny little thing. She had a puffy face, a squashed head and sunken eyes, and her little body was shaken with awful, terrifying fits," recalls Wendy.

Ka Yee was with them less than a year. One day she was distressed and crying. The puffiness of her face and limbs was increasing. After worrying and watching over her all day they took her to the clinic. Even the doctor found it hard to tell if Ka Yee was having fits or not. But it was then that the extent of the problems with her kidneys was diagnosed. Back at the Home she was administered careful doses of anti-convulsants and steroids. It seemed only a matter of time before her kidneys totally gave up. The doctor warned that her death might be extremely painful, so much prayer was made that her earthly end would be peaceful. She spent her last few weeks at the British Military Hospital.

"We used to go in every day to see her. There was a new chaplain at the hospital and we were so touched that he made a point of visiting her every day, too," says Wendy.

"Pui Yee went often, and usually sat by her bedside reading Bible verses out loud. Gradually Ka Yee got less and less alert. Eventually I got a call one late June evening to go to the ward – although, as the sister said, it was Pui Yee that needed me more than little Ka Yee.

"Arriving late at the hospital I found Ka Yee resting in a little bean bag chair that she was put on to prevent bedsores. Pui Yee and I took her down to the hospital chapel and sang, prayed, and cuddled her for the last time. She died at about 3.30am."

There remains another of those hard and hesitant question marks. Wouldn't it have been better for Ka Yee's mother to have bowed to pressure and had that abortion?

That begs an even wider debate. What about deliberately preventing the arrival into this world of a handicapped child? Modern technology has given the medical profession the ability to pinpoint many handicaps in the womb. Isn't abortion of the imperfect foetus the answer?

It's a suggestion that both Valerie and Wendy strongly reject.

"Handicapped children are born as they are because of mankind's sin," explains Valerie.

"Because of Adam and Eve's disobedience in the Garden of Eden, sin entered the perfect world God had created. And so we must expect today to see the results of sin. The handicapped baby is just part of that. And yet God made life sacred and precious and He has not allowed us to take life. Only God can take life, and if He decides to take the life of a handicapped baby then there will be a natural miscarriage."

Valerie is opposed even to the use of the word 'abortion', as she asserts it is covering up the reality that what is really meant is 'murder'.

"The only possible right time for taking the life of an unborn child would be if the mother's life was at risk – and even then it's a decision that can only properly be made with the Lord's guidance.

"Christian parents can look at the arrival of a retarded baby positively and with joy. A handicapped child can be a great blessing."

Wendy has similarly strong views. "A society that has only so-called perfect people would in fact be a very imperfect community. Unbalanced. Because if we are talking about removing the disabled or apparently useless then we are not just talking about the retarded child. We are talking about the elderly, the alcoholic, the drug addict. Where do you come to an end of deciding just who is of worth to the community?

"There is a difference between understanding with the eyes and with the heart. So many who could be put in the category of 'useless' to society are in fact precious to those who love them. Our children at the Home are priceless. I believe there is no one in the world unwanted – but often the right link between that person and the one who wants to love him is not made.

"No, all imperfect people have their place. They bring to our society a balance between selfishness and unselfishness, between acceptance and rejection. They make demands which stretch people – and that's good."

Wendy describes how very angry she was over the fuss made of "E.T", the outer-space creature hallowed by film, book and gimmick some years ago.

"These people buying ghastly, weird little E.T.s for their children to cuddle were the same people who would not pick up someone else's child who was deformed, and who wouldn't want their children to see him, to be near him, who definitely would not welcome such a child in their families.

"What kind of double standard is it to encourage your

child to make a pet and a treasured thing out of this horrible little monster of man's devising – but to look at a terribly deformed child and say 'Whatever is God thinking of?'"

Caring for the handicapped costs a great deal of money. Isn't this bad management of society's available resources?

"Are valuable resources really spent wrongly on the handicapped?" challenges Wendy. "What about money spent on space exploration or nuclear weapons?

"I am totally against spending money on sending a man to the moon while people on earth are in need. People talk of the need to achieve. There is still so much to achieve here on earth! We need to concentrate more on helping others to achieve. If we can help the elderly achieve; if we can help the alcoholic achieve – how much more valuable these things are than putting a man on the moon. The day that Thomas finally lifted his head by himself – that was a really great achievement!"

It's a sentiment echoed by Pui Yee. "Why should we care about the handicapped? Well, today I might be nursing them – but tomorrow I might be one of them. Today I might be pushing a wheelchair – tomorrow I might be sitting in one. Who knows? The handicapped have a right to dignity. God alone knows the true value of a person, handicapped or otherwise. Only he can take a life."

CHI KEUNG

The very same week that Ka Yee was admitted, another little one was admitted to the Home with an altogether more hopeful prognosis.

For some time Wendy had been following the case of a young boy with Downs syndrome, Chi Keung. His parents were very young and unable to care for him, so he was made a ward of court. His stay in hospital was prolonged by the need for major heart surgery and subsequent wound infection. Wendy kept in touch with his progress and visited him in the isolation ward.

She fell in love with the smiling boy, and they told the social worker that they would take him as soon as he could be discharged.

Fifteen months old, small and still bottle fed, Chi Keung was from the start perhaps the most "cuddly" of their children. Possibly deprived of security and human warmth in hospital, here he found a constant succession of "aunties" willing to pick him up and make a fuss of him as soon as he raised his arms to them. His cot was filled with the softest of furry toys, which he loved to cuddle, kiss and attempt to dress. From the start he had excellent fine motor control – he could pick up and manipulate even small objects.

At first, though, there was no rough and tumble. The scars from his surgery were still tender. His wariness of men in general or anyone wearing a white coat they attributed to an aversion to the many doctors he had encountered in his short life.

When he was old enough, Chi Keung was taken first to a playgroup and then to the same Baptist kindergarten that Daniel had attended. His first term was positive and happy. But the second term proved more difficult – his favourite teacher and his special friend Ricky both left and Chi Keung didn't always feel too good, suffering a succession of colds and other minor ailments. His speech didn't seem to be developing and he was given inconclusive hearing tests. Wendy and Valerie wondered if he had just learned to "switch off" in hospital. Certainly one of the disturbing things about him was that he often didn't cry when he was hurt – as if he had learned that it wouldn't do any good, that no one would come to comfort him.

Chi Keung became rather rebellious. Perhaps he worked out that refusing to eat created a lot of extra attention. Busy staff would spend a long time cuddling him, cajoling him with tasty titbits on spoons. It was a testing time for everyone. And perhaps the biggest trial was a number of "false" starts to adoption. Over a period of a year and a half several families showed an interest in adopting Chi Keung. But for one reason or another every possibility fell through, leaving the staff of the Home distressed and prayerful.

One of the volunteer workers occasionally took Chi Keung home for weekends as part of the plan to "break" him of his obstinate habit of refusing to eat properly and to give him some individual stimulus as part of a "normal" family.

And it was during these visits that Chi Keung met another family – the one that was to become his.

Gregory, in medical work at the Chinese University, and Helen, an experienced nanny and kindergarten teacher, had not been married long. They had separately left their native England to pursue their careers in Hong Kong. There they met at a church fellowship and fell in love. Within a year of their marriage they had a little son, Joshua – known as "J.J.".

They talked about having a second child soon. But then they met Chi Keung – and couldn't help but love him. To their delight, one-year-old "J.J." and three-year-old Chi Keung developed an immediate affinity, following each other around and giggling together over their own private jokes. Gregory and Helen prayerfully decided to postpone having another baby in favour of adopting Chi Keung. All the paperwork was signed for the six months probationary period the day before they were special guests at the 25th anniversary celebrations for the Home held in October 1990. With the signing of the adoption papers in April 1991 Chi Keung, almost five years old, officially became Nathan.

TWENTY-FIVE

The Love Goes On

When six-year-old Thomas died traumatically in hospital in early 1989, it was quite some months before the grieving staff could consider taking in a child to fill the empty cot.

A new admission was, as always, a matter of much prayer. There were so many on the waiting list and their true situations had to be assessed and weighed carefully.

Eventually it was decided to take in Wai Ching, whose tiny doll-like frame belied her 34 years.

Wai Ching had for some time been living in an old people's home, her mother being too elderly to care for her. She could walk if carefully led but was very nervous and dependent. She was visited frequently by her brother, Joseph, a Christian who had in the past been a volunteer cook at the Home of Loving Faithfulness. The first time anyone knew that Joseph had a retarded sister was when a couple from his church who were supporters of the Home mentioned it in a letter. The Home, they wrote, would be the ideal situation for Wai Ching, but they recognised that with so many claims on a limited number of places "it would take a miracle for her to be admitted".

The staff at the Home followed Wai Ching's progress as Joseph told them of her very distressing eye infections, which led to the complete loss of sight in one eye. Concerned about the lack of personal attention Wai Ching was receiving, one of the Home's volunteers, a lovely, caring Japanese woman called Yumi, took the trouble to travel to the Tsuen Mun old people's home each week to give her a wash, cut her nails, wash her hair and take her for a walk.

Then Joseph announced that after prayerful thought

he was applying to become a prison warder with Hong Kong's Correctional Services. He was accepted and began the very demanding training, with the staff at the Home keeping in touch and giving him encouragement.

Wendy remembers, "Some time after Tom's death we began to follow up on several names on our waiting list. Pui Yee felt strongly that we should take Wai Ching. I found her quite unprepossessing. But the sentence from that letter kept coming back to me – that it would take a 'miracle' for Wai Ching to be accepted. We could be the means of bringing about that miracle. And I thought of the benefits to Joseph if we should take his sister. He was a godly man wanting to serve the Lord." After some inner wrestling both Valerie and Wendy agreed with Pui Yee's longing to take Wai Ching. Having decided, they could think of little but how excited Joseph would be at the news.

Pui Yee called him. Suppressing her joy, she put on a casual voice, while Wendy and Valerie hovered around the phone grinning. She asked him if he would do some driving for the Home on his next day off – not an unusual request. When he agreed, she said that they wanted a new admission to be collected and measured for new clothes.

As Pui Yee gave him all the details, he didn't suspect a thing!

"Oh, Joseph, I suppose I'd better give you the name of the child. It's Wai Ching".

He was speechless with happiness.

WING YAN

Wing Yan was the Valentine's Day baby that came to the Home of Loving Faithfulness as a Christmas gift.

Two or three weeks before Christmas 1989, Valerie and Wendy had been thinking about babies a lot. They were due to occupy the new building soon. Should they think about using the smaller rooms in the old building for taking in babies? They discussed renovating a section for twelve cots. Babies were a lot more vulnerable and needed more careful nursing. But the good news was that an experienced missionary doctor was coming to live at the Home and would provide some medical cover for the children in return for accommodation.

So when they had a phone call referring to them the case of a tiny hydrocephalic baby girl, Valerie and Wendy were immediately interested and visited her in hospital. They called her social worker the next morning to say they would take her. If the paperwork was completed quickly, Wing Yan would be an extra-special Christmas gift to the Home.

Wing Yan had been born on February 14 that year into a family that already had many problems. It had been an arranged marriage, and the husband quickly discovered that his wife was mentally very unstable. Two children were born, after which the wife's condition had deteriorated and she now spent most of her time in hospital, diagnosed as schizophrenic. The arrival of a third child with mental retardation was a tremendous burden for the husband, a genuinely caring though naively simple man who was already struggling on very low wages to cope with the upbringing of the two other children, now nine and ten years old.

So Wing Yan had never left the hospital where she had been born. Apart from hydrocephalus, she had suffered a cardiac arrest at 20 days old, and she had anaemia. Although very tiny and pale, her trunk and thin limbs looked perfectly formed. Her little head had a squashed look to it, resulting in rather lopsided eyes and ears, and the fontanelles on her skull had never properly closed over. However, no Christmas gift could have been received with more joy and enthusiasm! All the staff found it hard to resist popping into the room where lay their new baby girl in the white wooden cot.

Wing Yan's story has only just begun as this book nears

its close. She's a little girl with great potential. Given lots of love and stimulation, who knows what tremendous future is in store for her? Physically, there's no reason why those thin legs should not walk. Medical expectations apart, there's no limit to the way God can deal with her limitations. One thing's certain. Whatever hope can be given to her in the form of loving care, will be given.

LIK WAI

God can bring something good out of something terrible. For Valerie and Wendy would never have met and loved Lik Wai if Thomas had not been on the hospital ward where he tragically died.

Lik Wai, like Thomas, was born a normal, healthy baby. But at the age of two a brain tumour was diagnosed, of a type that could not be completely surgically removed. Over the years a number of operations were performed to reduce the growing mass of tumour which gradually took from him his senses and abilities.

Lik Wai was convalescing after one of these surgeries on the same ward as Thomas. Wendy and Valerie were drawn to him because he was about the same age as Thomas and was suffering increasing mental disabilities. He was blind and unable to walk by then.

After Thomas died there was some disability allowance which the Home didn't want to claim from the Government. But when pressed by the social worker Valerie and Wendy wondered if they could give the money to help Lik Wai. They established contact with the family and bought them a wheelchair for their son. They were not a desperately poor family – father had a small printing factory – but providing the wheelchair was a great help. Soon a good relationship was formed with the family. Lik Wai's mother was very positive, always eager to find ways to help him.

In 1990 further surgery was carried out to reduce the

tumour mass, but this was followed by haemorrhaging. The family were told that there would be no more operations. The hospital had done all they could.

Lik Wai's deterioration accelerated. His speech dwindled to nothing and physically he was virtually helpless.

With Chi Keung's cot empty after he had gone to live with his new family, the staff felt they should take in Lik Wai for his remaining days to relieve the burden from his family. His parents were not Christians and those at the Home had been praying that they would come to know Jesus as Lord.

Lik Wai's mother visited almost daily and, being so used by now to life on a hospital ward, made herself very useful not just with her own son but the other children. Lik Wai continued to slip away from this world, soon needing to be tube fed, and causing no small anxiety on several occasions when he had raging fevers.

However, he held his own until the night of 13th March, 1991. Then, sensing that the end was really near, Wendy called a doctor and summoned the parents at 3am. Father had to leave the bedside at 7.15am to go to work, but mother stayed on and Lik Wai died peacefully an hour later.

Wendy says, "We carried him to the chapel where members of the family could come and see him. His mother had bought him a new suit at Christmas which he had never been able to wear, also new sneakers, so we dressed him in those. He was a beautiful big child with lovely skin.

"Many came to the funeral and we buried him on the hill overlooking the Home. There were many tears, especially from his father at the graveside."

The staff of the Home are continuing their loving support of the family. Just as there's fruit after the dying of the seed, so they pray there will be spiritual fruit there in time.

Helping others cope with bereavement is a loving speciality of the Home. But how do the staff themselves come to terms with the deaths of the children and adults they have cared for so intimately, often for many years?

"When we know that we are going to lose a child our first feelings are to pray that the child goes peacefully and that they know that they are going to the Lord Jesus, where they will be perfect," says Valerie.

"We read them Scriptures even though we don't know how much they understand. The point of dying is rather beautiful because we know that we are handing them on to a perfect life where they will become the beings they were intended to be. Generally it's a peaceful transition.

"Of course there is sadness, as if some part of us has been lost. Being busy makes it perhaps easier. And there are always new children coming on whom you need to expend your love even when you are feeling that something special has gone from you.

"This is perhaps not as difficult to cope with as the loss of a loved one whom you are not sure knows the Lord, when there may be feelings of guilt and distress as you don't know if they are in the Kingdom or not. But we have no fear about the destiny of our children."

Knowing that many of the children have a poor prognosis and may die suddenly is neither consolation nor preparation, though, for the shock of actual death, insists Wendy.

"When you have cared for and nursed someone moving towards death, every day you are living with the knowledge of death just around the corner. You think of how you will cope but you are having to live with that person in a natural, normal way — sort of living a double life. That's tremendously draining. Some illnesses which a normal child would come through can be fatal to our brain-damaged children, while other chronic conditions which would threaten a normal, healthy person, such as fevers or continual vomiting, our children survive.

"So when an acute condition occurs we think about

death and if it's a time of trauma and distress for the child we pray for God's will to be done although physically we do all we can to deal with the problem, treating the condition and bringing relief without going to the extreme measures of having them on life-support for months on end.

"But all the time you are carrying death around inside you while trying to be positive for their sake, so that when the death comes you are actually so worn down that it really hurts. We know that many people are surprised to see this happen. Sometimes in a family Mum concentrates all her efforts into the handicapped child and afterwards people say, 'Well, she knew that child wouldn't live for long. Why is she in this condition?' But that mother has been trying to make her child's experience full of life.

"I remember when Susie was in Ruttonjee Hospital for a long time - about 11 months. One time I met Sister Gabriel on the ward and she said to me, 'You have to realise that Susie is dying.' I nearly attacked her physically, much as I love her. I said, 'Susie's not dying – she's living!' because I was so afraid that if they all looked at her as if she was dying then everything around her would be dying instead of alive. The last part of her life would be so negative; maybe people would even stop doing things for her."

A sense of bereavement can also hit you when you know the person hardly at all, says Wendy.

"I've grieved over two children on our waiting list that I longed to take but we were not able. Both died and I experienced something like having a miscarriage. My arms felt empty because I'd never held them."

TWENTY-SIX

A Footnote on the Future

Unlike this book, the story of the Home of Loving Faithfulness has no end. As we write, Chi Keung, now Nathan, is just beginning a whole new life in his adopted family, making exciting progress in speech therapy. The death of dear Charlotte, Valerie's giggly teenage daughter, is still a too-fresh grief.

And what of the latest newcomers? Yuk Lan has been taken in: a little girl of 15 months with spina bifida, hydrocephalus, a hare lip and cleft palate. Like Wing Yan, "she's cute, bright – and, in our eyes, definitely adoptable" report Valerie and Wendy. And after her came three-year-old Wai Mui. She's blind and has multiple handicaps, but also "beautiful big eyes and a mass of long dark hair".

Then in May 1991 came 12-year-old Yin Fan, extremely physically handicapped but mentally normal. Yin Fan suffers from a condition known as dystoria musculorum deformans and her prognosis is poor.

And the following month the Home took in the baby Wendy had dreamed of, but never believed would exist.

"Ever since I'd known Daniel I'd prayed to God that if there was ever any other limbless child in Hong Kong, He would give him to us to love and care for." What joy it was for her to take in Dat Vinh, the four-month-old limbless baby born to a young couple in one of the city's Vietnamese refugee camps. Dat Vinh, known as Benjamin, is making good progress.

The children keep coming and the love goes on. This chronicle has recorded something of the Home's first 25 years. By God's grace there will be many more years.

Hong Kong is currently overshadowed by the uncertainty of the 1997 handover to Chinese dominion. The late 80s and early 90s have been marked by swelling tides of emigration to the West. Sadly, many churches and Christian organisations in the colony are losing key people to the United States, Canada, Australia or Britain. The Sino-British agreement allows for a 50-year transitional period of "one country – two systems". The impact on the Christian community of the change in government cannot be adequately forecast – but some fear the worst.

Both Valerie and Wendy are adamant in their commitment to Hong Kong, which has been their home for 30 years.

"We shall stay on after 1997, because this is the work that God has given us to do and he hasn't told us to go. How could we leave these children who are our family and our responsibility?" says Valerie.

"As for us personally in regard to the running of the Home – as we get older, we know that our abilities are decreasing; so we pray for the Lord to send someone to take over."

Unsurprisingly Wendy affirms, "It's my hope to remain always in Hong Kong. I've no desire to live anywhere else. We are confident that God has a plan for the future of the Home.

"1997 is likely to affect the Home financially – we are expecting that it may be a hard time. However, that is no great concern as we know the God who has always met our needs will continue to do so".

Whatever poverty comes to Hong Kong – poverty of freedom, of people and resources – Valerie and Wendy intend, by the grace of God, that the Home of Loving Faithfulness will always be a place of riches. Certainly, many have found it so. Here is a wealth of love and care; here is an abundance of trust, faith and prayer. The "love to the loveless shown that they might lovely be" is overwhelming in its power and beauty.

"Some missionaries have suggested we are wasting our time on our children. They say we would be more profitable for God if we were evangelising or teaching," says Wendy.

"And there have been times through the years when we have felt inadequate that we are not out there in the needy world pushing people into the Kingdom of God.

"But the children we care for are not the end. They are a means of glorifying God.

"Even the fact that we as a family live by faith in God testifies to His glory, His love, His faithfulness. Through our Home the lives of many have been blessed and encouraged.

"In Isaiah 45 verse 3 God gives this promise: 'I will give you the treasures of darkness, riches stored in secret places, so that you may know that I am the Lord, the God of Israel, who summons you by name.'

"These words are so relevant to our work and our calling. Our children are a secret, unexpected place to find riches. You don't always easily see these wonderful riches. You have to break the code. The riches are hidden – but they're there. And when you do see them, it's a privilege. It's something very precious."

The Home of Loving Faithfulness
7 Castle Peak Road
Kwu Tung
Sheung Shui
New Territories
Hong Kong